COMPILED BY MEMBE...

ANGLO-SCO...
FAMILY HISTORY SOCIETY

A DICTIONARY OF
SCOTTISH
EMIGRANTS
VOL.2

PUBLISHED BY

MANCHESTER & LANCASHIRE FAMILY HISTORY SOCIETY

Clayton House

59 Piccadilly

Manchester

MI 2AQ

© January 1988

ISBN   0 947701 30 3

i

CONTENTS

PLACE-NAMES have been transcribed as accurately as possible, but
it should be remembered that Census enumerators and others would
have difficulty in spelling these strange sounding names, as we
often have in deciphering them. A gazetteer could be helpful in
tracking down locations.

INTRODUCTION

The first dictionary of emigrant Scots was totally dedicated to
those whose birthplace in Scotland was known, with the remaining
being kept as an index file. As this index grew it became
evident that a great majority of Scots were only known as "born
in Scotland", even so there was still a wealth of information in
these files as they showed family units, occupations and the
areas favoured by Scots in which to settle. As this index was
not easily accessible to members, it was decided to include the
entries in this second volume. Therefore this edition is
divided into two sections, the first is dedicated to Scots whose
birthplace in Scotland is known, and the second to those who are
known only as "born in Scotland". It is hoped that as members
find their Scottish origins they will send in updated
contributions and then their ancestors can be "promoted" to the
first section. In addition an index has been included, these
are people who are mentioned in the dictionary, but are either
not Scottish or have not been given a main heading in their own
right. Amongst these are English spouses whose maiden name is
known, other relatives and lodging house keepers etc.

May I take this opportunity to thank everyone who has
contributed to this volume and whose continued enthusiasm has
ensured the publication of several more. It is hoped that
members will note any Scots they come across during their own
researches in records and send them to the society, they will be
very gratefully received and included in future dictionaries or
used to expand information already known. When sending in
census information, could members please include the complete
family unit when ever possible, as amongst other things this can
give a picture of the movement of the family from the children's
places of birth and relatives such as "in laws" are often found
at the same address.

Finally my thanks go to Mr. J.D. Beckett, Chairman, and Mrs.
D.F. Ramsbotham, Secretary, for continually funnelling the
information in my direction, and to my mother Mrs. D.H. Dixon,
whose help in sifting through the hundreds of files has been
invaluable. Also special thanks to my brother, Mr. V.W. Dixon,
for the use of his computer, which has helped reduce a mammoth
task to a more workable level.

V.L. Dixon

Projects Secretary

iv

ADIE James M. 1881 census Westoe and Jarrow, Co Durham, St. Marks. 117 Adelaide St. Married 47 years old, seaman, born Shetland.

ALDER John born 1st June 1806, baptised 6th November 1808. 1st son of Thomas Alder, shipwright, native of Pallion and Barbara, his wife, late HENDERSON, native of North Caithness. Bishopwearmouth, Co Durham, Baptisms.

ALDER Ralph born 22nd June 1808, baptised 6th November 1808, 2nd son of Thomas Alder, details as above.

ALEXANDER George 32 years, born Huntley, Aberdeenshire. Living at Newby, North Yorkshire, 1851, with his wife Ann, 31 years and two children, Charles 3 years and Elizabeth 1 year, all born Newby, North Yorkshire. Reel HO107/2376 folio 144.

ALEXANDER 1851 census, Carlisle, Cumb., Botchergate, 49 Saddle Lane. James R. Alexander, head, married, 23 years, last maker. Ann, wife, 22 years, shoe maker. Both born Edinburgh.

ALLAN Christian, relict of James CARRICK Esq. of Meadow Park, Nr. Glasgow. Died 18th September 1839 age 81 years. St. James, Liverpool, Necropolis, Nonconformists.

ALLARDICE Christian, 1881 census, Stokesley, North Riding of Yorkshire. Widow, 73 years, born Berick, Scotland.

ALLCHIN Jane, 1851 census, Northallerton. 62 years born Ayr. Reel HO 107/2377 folio 352.

ALSTON James, born 4 June 1744 at Redsyde, East Lothian. Died Winson Hill, Wks. 18th October 1827. M.I. from Smethwick Old Church, Staffs.

ANDERSON Christian, wife of George HENRY, see HENRY for details.

ANDERSON George, born 15th September 1802, baptised 31st October 1802, 3rd son of George Anderson, bottle maker, native of Ayrs Quay by his wife Elizabeth TURNS, native of Alloa, North Britain. St. Hilda, South Shields, Co Durham, Baptisms.

ANDERSON William 3rd son of David Anderson of Bandoch, Forfarshire, Scotland. Drowned while bathing in the Mersey 7th June 1835 in his 14th year. St. James, Liverpool, the Necropolis, nonconformists.

ANDREWS 1851 census Bolton. 2 Kynuster Yard or Rynuster. Thomas Andrews, 58 years, weaver, born army? Brit. Sub. Euphema, wife, 62 years, born Argyleshire, Scotland. Reel 14 2211 If folio 186a

ATKINSON Elias, 19 years, unmarried, groom, born Glasgow. 1851 census Bolton. Hoker Fold, Darcy Lever. Reel 2211 3cb, folio 709a.

AUCKINCLOSE Ruth, 14years, born Paisley, Scotland. 1851 census
Broughton, North Yorkshire, folio 41

BARLOW Jane wife of James Barlow, a private in the Royal
Artillary, born 11th December 1782, baptised and received 16th
October 1808, 1st daughter of William BROWN, reelman, native of
this parish and Jane, his wife late GILCHRIST, native of
Glasgow. Bishopwearmouth, Co Durham, baptisms.

BATES Benigma? born July 1805 baptised 28th July 1805,
illegitimate dau of James BATES shoe maker, native of Rothbury,
Northumberland, by his wife Eleanor BIRD, native of Preston
Pans, East Lothian. St. Hildas, South Shields, baptisms.

BAXTER Mary formerly of the Custom House, Greenock, died at Holt
Hill, Birkenhead, Cheshire, 12th August 1847 age 65 years.
Following children of Archibald Baxter, Jessie Ralston died 4th
July 1855 an infant, Archibald Neil Leitch died 6th March 1856,
infant. St. James, Liverpool, the Necropolis, noncomformists.

BAYNES William, 47 years, clog last maker, born Dumfries, living
at 6 Birketts Ct. Whitehaven. Holy Trinity, 1851 census. With
his wife Cath 40years, born Hull and step son John WHITE 17
years, born Chelsea.

BELL Benjamin eldest son of George Bell, surgeon, of Edinburgh
and grandson of Benjamin Bell of Hunthill, Roxburghshire, died
at Ramsey June 11th 1843, aged 42 years. M.I.(85), St. Mary's
Chapel, Ballure, Ramsey, Isle of Man. From Isle of Man FHS.

BELL Mary relict of John GUNNING, see Gunning for details.

BELL Robert, 16 years, born Inverness, Scotland. 1851 census
Northallerton. Reel HO 107/2377, folio 338.

BELL Thomas Esqr, late of Kirkcaldy, ship owner, died 16th
January 1842 (60). From " Liverpool Epitaphs " MSS, J. Gibson,
vol. 5. Scotch Church, Rodney Street. (Presb) Ref. L'pl record
office H929 GIB.

BENNENGALL Elizabeth, born 23rd July 1803 baptised 27th June
1805, 1st son(?) of George Bennengall, cordwainer, native of
Edinburgh by his wife Sarah PATTISON, native of this place. St.
Hildas, South Shields, Co Durham, baptisms.

BENNET Margaret, 1st daughter of John Bennet, brewer, native of
Morebattle, Roxburghshire, by his wife Margaret, dau. of Henry
DURHAM, native of Lamesley, Co Durham. Born 6th May 1812,
baptised 17th May 1812. St. John's, Newcastle upon Tyne,
baptisms.

BENNIS living at Winwick Street, Warrington, 1851 Census. John
Bennis, 65 years, retired superintendant habber? of Glasgow,
born New Kilpatrick, Stirlingshire. Isabell 63 years, wife, born
Pollokshaws, Renfrew. Robert 20 years, son, assist. land
surveyor, born Glasgow.

BIRD Eleanor and Benigma? see BATES Benigma? for details.

BLACK Margaret, born 2nd October 1803, baptised 30th October
1803, 1st dau. of James Black, cordwainer, native of Dunbar, by
his wife Jane UNION native of Perth, Scotland. St. Hilda's,
South Shields, Co Durham, baptisms.

BLAIR Catherine, 18 years, servant, born Castle Douglas. 1851
Census, Carlisle. Reel HO/2430, folio 228.

BLAKE living at 16 Green Street, Westoe and Jarrow, Durham. 1881
census. St. Marks Parish. Thomas S. Blake, married, 47 years,
Police Constable, born Newcastle, Northumberland. Esther, wife,
39 years, born Edinburgh, Scotland. Children, Esther, 14 years,
domestic servant. Thomas S., 13 years. Mary A., 11 years.
George, 9 years. Katherine, 7 years. Dorah, 5 years. Sarah E., 4
years. Jane E., 3 years. James, 6 months, all born South
Shields, Co. Durham.

BLYTH Charles son to David Blyth of Dalkeithing in ye Kingdom of
Scotland, a stranger, baptised 7th March and buried 10th March
1741/2. Earsden (by North Shields) Co Northumberland.

BLYTHE George, 29 years, curriers journeyman, born Edinburgh.
Lodging with Sarah Hunt, widow. 1851 census Stokesley, North
Riding Yorkshire. Reel HO 107/2376.

BONNER living at Leadbetter Fold, Little Lever, Bolton. 1851.
Isabella Bonner, 38 years, born Leath, Scotland. Jane, dau., 13
years, born Carlisle. William, son, 11 years, born Carlisle.
John, son, 8 years, born Leath, Scotland. Isabella, dau., 2
years, born Bolton, Little Lever. Reel 2211 2Db folio 639a.

BOOKLESS living at Wimbledon Hill Road, Wimbledon, Surrey. 1881.
James P. Bookless, head, widower, 35 years, Doctor of Medicine
in practice, born Kelso, Scotland. Jane H.P., mother, widow, 66
years, born Kelso. Mary J., sister, unmarried, 30 years, born
Kelso. From Essex FHS.

BOWHILL John born 24th March 1805, baptised 1st May 1808, 1st
son of John Smith Bowhill, native of Kelso, Scotland, and Ann
his wife, late MITCHELL, native of Haughton le Spring.
Bishopwearmouth, Co Durham, baptisms.

BOWHILL Ann born 5th April 1808, baptised 1st May 1808, 1st dau.
of John Smith Bowhill, details as above.

BOYES living at Rindle, Astley, Lancs. 1871 census. Joseph
Boyes, 61 years, agr. labourer, born Dumfries. Elizabeth, wife,
64 years, born Dumfries. Joseph, son, 33 years, born Dumfries.
John, son, 23 years, born Astley, Lancs.

BROWN Jane, wife of James BARLOW, see BARLOW Jane for details.

BROWN David of Torryburn, Fifeshire. Died July 13th 1857, age 40
years. M.I. St. Michael and All Saints Parish Church,
Lilleshall, Shropshire.

BROWN George born 28th December 1807, baptised 10th July 1808,
1st son of Thomas Brown, native of Haddington, Scotland, and
Francis his wife late, BENSON, native of Houghton le Spring.
Bishopwearmouth, Co Durham, baptisms.

BROWN Isabella late of Aberdeen, died 16th January 1849, age 48
years. Grave 683, St. Georges Church yard Castle Street,
Liverpool.

BROWN Jessie, wife of Samuel MAY, see MAY Thomas.

BROWN John, here lieth the body of John Brown merchant in
Liverpool, born in Galloway in Scotland of an ancient family of
that name there, who died the 19th February 1724. From
"Liverpool Epitaphs" J. Gibson MSS> Vol.1 M.I.s in St. Peter's
Churchyard (C of E) L'pl. Rec. Office ref. H929 GIB.

BROWN Margaret born 25th February 1802 baptised 31st July 1803,
5th dau. of John Brown, mariner, native of Farfur, Angnes, by
his wife, Margaret COCKERILL, native of Scarboro. St. Hilda's,
South Shields, Co Durham, baptisms.

BROWN William of Kirkcudbright, North Britain, who departed this
life - age - William Brown - - February 1788 age 85 years. Grave
47 St Peter's, Church Street, Liverpool.

BROWN William born 26th August 1803? baptised 2nd January 1803,
1st son of John Brown, mariner of Forfar, North Britain, by his
wife Margaret COCKERILL native of Scarboro. St. Hilda's, South
Shields, Co Durham, baptisms.

BRUCE Annie wife of William COW and mother of Ann MACDONALD, see
MACDONALD Ann for details.

BRUCE Barbara native of Aberdeenshire died in Liverpool 15th
January 1826 age 60 years. Monument placed by W. B. SANGSTER for
his mother. William Bruce Sangster born 15th October 1800 died
7th August 1862, Annie Bruce dau. of W.B. Sangster died 8th
January 1848, Elizabeth Bruce, also his dau. born at Winsford
Lodge 14th December 1852, died at Edgbaston 25th December
1852.St. James Liverpool, Necropolis, noncomformists.

BRUNTON William born Lochwinnoch, Ayrshire, 26th May 1777. Died
Camborne, Cornwall 5th October 1851 age 74 years. Biographical
Dictionary of Railway Engineers.

BULLIVANT Ann, 70 years, mangler, born Aberdeen. Living at 64
Howard Place. 1851 St. Philip, Birmingham, census, EN 9 sch 87
page 279.

BURNS Ann, relict of James E. SHAIN, teacher of languages, Perth
Scotland, died 19th February 1870 age 76 years. Thomas his son
died 26th April 1856 age 19 years, Eliza dau. of above and wife
of James McCURRICH, died 18th Jan 1877 age 62 years. Grave 1621A
St. Georges Churchyard, Castle Street, Liverpool.

BRYDEN Archibald 34 years, traveller and tea dealer, born Lochmaben, Scotland, visitor in household of William KERR see KERR. 16 West Street, Poole area, Dorset, 1851 census.

CAMPBELL Hugh, 75 years, labourer, born Twinan, Scotland. Living at Straits, Astley, Lancs. 1871 census, with Hannah, wife, 70 years, born Worsley.

CAMPBELL I. K. surgeon of Aberdeen, erected memorial to the memory of his brother in law William THOMPSON, M.D. of H.M. 13th Dragoons, died Liverpool 21st May 1831 on return from the West Indies age 30 years. Ref Liverpool record office H 929 GIB

CAMPBELL Samuel James born Glasgow 5th June 1836 died Warroad 16th October 1919 Minnisota. U.S.A. obituaries, Sun Chronical, Rhode Island.

CAMPBELL William born 8th August 1804 baptised 8th October 1804, 2nd son of John Campbell, mariner, native of Leith, North Britain by his wife Elizabeth JEFFELS native of this place. St. Hilda's, South Shields, Co Durham, baptisms.

CARMICHAEL Mary 27 years unmarried, domestic servant, born Dumfrieshire, Scotland. 34 Paradise Street, Birmingham. 1851 census En. 5 sch. 5. page 131 Reel H.O. 107/2055

CARRICK James husband of Christian ALLAN see ALLAN Christian for details.

CAY Mary, wife of George DAVIE, see DAVIE William for details.

CHAPPELL living at Disley, Cheshire. 1881 census. William Chappell, 41 yrs. print works, born Pendleton, Lancs. Margaret, wife, 40 yrs. born Glasgow. Children, Robert, 20 yrs. Mary, 18 yrs. James, 16 yrs. George, 14 yrs. Agnes, 11 yrs. Samuel, 9 yrs. Fred, 5 yrs. Gilbert, ?yrs.

CHISHOLM Jennet, wife of John CHISHOLM, port Glasgow, shipmaster, and dau. of John and Cath LAIRD died at Gateshead of consumption. No. 245 20th December 1831 Ward H No. 24. age 33 years. Westgate Cem., Elswick, Newcastle upon Tyne. Interments.

CHRISTIE living at Barn Street, Bolton. 1851 census. James Christie 54 years, iron moulder, born Stirling, Scotland, Ellen, wife, 53 years, born Stirling, Phillip, son 14 years, born Bolton, Charles, son, 11 years, born Bolton. Reel 14 2211 Io folio 516a.

CHRISTIE living at 81 Spring Gardens, Bolton 1851 census. William Christie 29 years, iron moulder, born Stirling, Scotland, Mirrian, wife, 31 years, born Glasgow, Janet, dau, 5 years, born Bolton, Alexander, son, 2 years, born Bolton. Reel 2211 In folio 486a.

CLARK living in Northallerton 1851 census. Alexander Clark, 21 years, born Kirkgill, Scotland. Ann, mother, 44 years, born, Kirkgill. Peter, father, 48 years, born Rupet, Perthshire, Scotland. Reel H O 107/2377.

CLEUGH Jane born 18th October 1802, baptised 14th November 1802, 2nd dau. of George Cleugh, mariner, native of Edinburgh by his wife Mary SCOTT, native of this place. St. Hilda's, South Shields, Co Durham, baptisms.

COATS Thomas born 25th July 1803, baptised 20th February 1803, 1st son of Thomas COATS, mariner, native of Shetland by his wife Jane TUTEN, native of Darlington. St. Hilda's, South Shields, Co Durham, baptisms.

COCHRAN Louisa Helen Gordon, dau. of J. R. Cochran of Calderglen Lanarkshire and wife of Harry Devereux HICKMAN, died 18th March 1951. M.I. from St. Mary Magdalene, Lillington, Wks.

COCKER James, son in law of James ROY, see ROY James.

COLLIES Ellen, 61 years in 1881, charwoman, born Glasgow. Wife of Joseph Collies, 50 years, house painter, born Manchester. Thomas Collies, son, 18 years, also born Manchester. Living at 3 Duke Street, Ancoats. 1881 census, Reel 2855, dist. 13.

COLTART Margaret, 18 years, servant, born Rerwick, Scotland. Knutsford Road, Preston Place, Warrington, 1851 census.

CONNELL Eleanor, born 22nd February 1803, baptised 18th November, 1804, 2nd dau. of Michael Connell, mariner, native of Cambletown, Argyllshire, by his wife Thomasine TINDLE, native of this place. St. Hilda's, South Shields, Co Durham, baptisms.

CONNELL Elizabeth, servant, unmarried, 38 years, born Perth, Scotland. Living in home of Thomas H. YORKE, see YORKE. 1851 census, Bishop Middleham, Co Durham. Reel 107/2384 folio 723.

COPELAND George born 28th August 1800, baptised 29th May 1803, 5th son of James Copeland native of Reeth by his wife Mary WRIGHT, native of this place.

COPELAND Nicholas born 16th January 1802, baptised 29th May 1803, 6th son of above. St. Hilda, South Shields.

COOPER Jane, mother of Jane WEBSTER and wife of Thomas WEBSTER. see WEBSTER Jane.

COPPIN Jane, wife of Frederick Coppin, see Jane WEBSTER for full details.

CORN Phillipine Eliza, born Glasgow 10th August 1834, died in Llangollen, North Wales 20th August 1846, erected by her parents. St. James, Liverpool, Necropolis, nonconformists.

COW William father of Ann MACDONALD, see MACDONALD Ann, for details.

COWELL living at Chorley, Lancs. 1851. Elizabeth Cowell, married, 32 years, visitor, born Milton of Campsie, Scotland. James, 5 months and Sarah, 5 years, both born Milton of Campsie. Reel 2263 folio 124.

COWIE George of Limekilns, North Britain, died 1/3/1873 age 33 years. Wife Catherine ADAMSON died 25/1/1871 age 31 years. Weaste cem. Salford. M.I. 954/33.

CRAIG living at 18 Smallbrook Street, Birmingham. 1851 census. James Craig, head, married 41 years, currier and leather seller, born Scotland, Dumfries. Susannah, wife, 41 years, born Scotland, Dumfries. St. Philip, B'ham 1851 census, en 7, sch 20 p216.

CREIGHTON Archibald 40 years, foreman joiner, born Maxwell? Scotland. Living with Sarah, wife, 40 years, born Shrewsbury. Mary dau. 15 years, Sarah, dau., 13 years, Archibald, son, 11 years, William, son, 8 years, and Margaret, dau. 7 years, all born Penketh. 1851 census Goldborn Street, Warrington.

CRICHTON Alexander, beloved son and brother born at Leith 3rd March 1822, died 28th February 1868, age 77 years, Anfield Cemetery, Liverpool.

CROCKER Elizabeth, 81 years, born Edinburgh, Scotland. South Tawton, Devon. 1851 census, reel H O 107/1885 folio 435.

CROOK living at Woodside Square, Darcy Lever, Bolton. Peter Crook, 55 years, weaver, born Bolton. Margaret, wife, 56 years, born Glasgow. 1851 census Bolton reel 2211 2Dc folio 664.

CROOKSHANK Jean, relict of the late Captain Robert Crookshank of Stromness, Orkney and mother of Mrs. Jean GEDDES, died 28th April 1832 age 77 years, latter buried here, died 10th July 1835, age 45. Relict of Captain John Geddes who died at sea 4th December 1832 age 44 years. Full entry pp. 261-265 vol.8 St. James Liverpool, the Necropolis, nonconformists.

CROSBIE Alexander, uumarried, 16 years, apprentice, born Dumfries. 1851 census Carlisle. Reel HO/2430, folio 223.

CRUICKSHANK Alexander late of Niekerbe, colony of Surinam., born in parish of Forgue (Torgue?) Scotland in 1800, died Liverpool 21st August 1838 after landing the previous day from New York. St. James, Liverpool.

CURRIE living at 9 Webster Street, All Souls, Manchester, 1851 census. Robert Currie 35, engine fitter, born Dumfries. Margaret 30 years, wife, born Inverness. Robert, son, 7 years, born Glasgow, Mary A.G. dau. 5years, born Glasgow. Cath VALS? 54years widow, mother in law, born Inverness. Reel HO 107/2226, page 673.

DAVIE William born 11th May 1807, baptised 20th November 1808, 1st son of George Davie, carpenter, native of Sunderland and Mary, his wife, late CAY, native of Stornaway, Scotland. Bishopwearmouth, Co Durham, baptisms.

DAVIDSON John a native of Roxborough died at Pershore 1st June 1837 aged 75 years. M.I. from St. James the Less, Bredicot, Worcs.

DAVY Mary wife of Charles, hawker, born Glasgow at Pinfold, Keighley, Yorkshire, 1881 census.

DEAN Christina Douglas Fairless widow of William Dean born Edinburgh 14th August 1826, died Knowle 25th May 1897 dau. of James WHITE, surgeon. M.I. from Knowle parish church, Warks.

DIXON Margaret born 19th February 1812, baptised 4th October 1812, 3rd dau. of Robert DIXON, blacksmith, native of Haddington, North Britain, by his wife Margaret dau of James HAY?, tanner, native of Edinburgh. St. John's, Newcastle upon Tyne, baptisms.

DON Frederick William Robertson born Forfar, Scotland 24th January 1888 died 28th November 1916. M.I. from St. James, Milverton, Warks.

DONALDSON James born 21st September 1745 at Perth, North Britain, Tayside. Died 18th October 1832, Abbey Foregate, Shrewsbury, where he resided 63 years, also Ann his wife died 9th January 1825 age 75 years. From M.I. Moreton Corbet, Shropshire.

DOUGAL Richard Ronay of Rothes, Midlothian and Balnageith, Morayshire died 10th April 1880 aged 59 years. M.I. from St. Mary Magdalene, Lillington, Wks.

DOUGLAS Ann born 1st August 1803, baptised 2nd October 1803, 1st dau. of William DOUGLAS, mariner, native of Dunsal, by his wife, Martha HUNTER, native of this place. St. Hilda's, South Shields. Co Durham, baptisms.

DOUGLAS James 19 years, born Gallowayshire, Scotland. 1851 census, Northallerton. Reel HO 107/2377 folio 342.

DOUGLAS Mary Ord born 25th November 1807, baptised 13th November 1808, 2nd dau. of William Douglas, private in the Glasgow volunteers and Ann, hid wife, late ORD, native of Peawsworth. Bishopwearmouth, Co Durham, baptisms.

DOUGLAS Robert died 15th May 1839 aged 31 years, native of Dumfries and late clerk in Liverpool dock offices for 12 years. Robert his son died 4th August 1836 age 5 months. St. James, Liverpool.

DREW Jane wife of James Drew late of Clemfeulen, Dumbartonshire and dau. of Thomas MUIR of Murrark, Lanarkshire died 19th April 1807 aged 45. M.I. St. James, Milverton, Warks.

DUNCAN James born 8th October 1802 baptised 18th October 1803,
2nd son of James Duncan, hairdresser, native of Aberdeen, North
Britain, by his wife Jane OLIVER, native of Newcastle upon Tyne.
St. Hilda's, South Shields, Co Durham, baptisms.

DUNCAN Thomas, head, widower, 72 years, music seller, born
Dunan, Scotland. Thomas I. son, unmarried, 37 years, organ
builderman, born Brentford, Middlesex. Living at 56 Market
Street, Poole area, Dorset. 1851 census.

DUNCAN William born 19th Sept. 1802, baptised 14th Aug. 1803,
3rd son of Alexander Duncan, native of Aberdeen, by his wife
Mary RAMSEY native of this place. St. Hilda's, South Shields.

DUNN Alex. 41 years, iron founder, born Coldstream. Living at 24
Tutbury Street, All Souls, Manchester. 1851 census. With
Elizabeth, 40 years, wife. Elizabeth, 11 years, dau. William
Thomas, 9 years, son. Richard Lyon, 7 years, son. Mary BOWERS,
64 years, widow, mother in law. Alex. Dunn 5 years, son. all
born Manchester. Reel HO 107/2226 page 671.

ELLIOT James, head, married, 45 years, agr. labourer, born
Dumfriesshire, Scotland. Living at Yanwath Moor. 1851
census.Yanwath, Eamont Bridge, Nr. Penrith, Cumb.

ELLIOTT Robert of Annandale, Scotland, died at Walsall 30th
November 1914, also his wife Dinah PATTINSON died at Dudley 3rd
March 1909. M.I. from King Street independent chapel, Dudley.

ELLIOT William M.D. born 6th August 1797, Kelso, Roxburghshire,
son of William Elliot, architect and Jean nee ROBERTSON. Married
Sarah Georgiana MILLER at St. Dunstans, Stepney, 20th April
1826. Children William born 1827, George born 1830, Gilbert
Stanley born 1832, Dunsterville born 1835, Jean born 1837,
Harvard born 1841, Mary born 1840, John born 1844, Edith born
1845. Died 23rd June 1869, Redhill, Surrey. Apprenticed to
William ROBERTSON of Kelso. Studied for M.D. at Edinburgh Royal
Infirmary, M.D. 1828, L.R.C.S. 1815, L.S.A. 1822. Practiced at
Stratford, Essex until 1869.

FAIRBAIRN William, 56 years, joiner, born Berwick, Scotland,
living at 68 Bradford Road, St. Phillips, Manchester, 1851
census. With Sarah, wife, 55 years, born Salop, Bishops Gate.
James, son, 19 years, joiners apprentice, born London, Christ
Church. Mary Sarah, dau., 12 years, born Manchester. William,
son, 26 years, married, book seller, born London. Elizabeth,
dau. in law, 28 years, pattern maker, born Armagh Ireland.
William David, grandson, 2 years, born Manchester. George HOWES,
27 years, married, visitor, weaver, born Cork. Sarah HOWES, 25
years, visitor, married, born Edinburgh. Reel HO/107/2226 page
726/726A.

FAIRRIE Charles Robert son of Adam and Margaret Fairrie,
formerly of Greenock, died 17th March 1850, aged 9 Months. Jane
their Dau. died 30th August 1856 age 13 years. Marianne their
youngest dau. Died 27th Feb. 1863 at Cannes, buried here.
Margaret JOHNSTON wife of Adam Fairrie died 8th August 1873 age

66 years. Adam Fairrie Died 26th July 1879 age 81 years. St.
James, Liverpool. Continuation of previous entry. For Margaret
their dau. see MOORE Margaret.

FARNIE Arthur late Bervie, North Britain, husband of Ann died
3/1/1920 age 70 years. Ann Valentine widow of above died
5/4/1932 in her 92nd year. Arthur Farnie J.P. died 10/3/1958 age
91 years. Peel Green Cem. Manchester.

FARRIE James, ship's master, native of Irvine, died 6th January
1843 age 49 years. James eldest son of above ship's master died
24th July 1850 age 30 years. "Liverpool Epitaphs" MSS J. Gibson,
Vol. 5 Scotch Church, Rodney Street. Ref. L'pl record office H
929 GIB.

FENWICK Margaret born 15th October 1803, baptised 25th December
1803, 1st dau. of George Fenwick, mariner, native of Stockton,
by his wife Margaret FINDLEY, native of Montrose, North Britain.
St. Hilda's South Shields, Co Durham, baptisms.

FERGUSON Ann wife of John Ferguson, teacher, Inch, Wigtownshire,
died 28th September 1851 age 40 years. Grave 545, St. Georges
Churchyard, Castle Street, Liverpool.

FERGUSON John born at Dunrobin, Sutherlandshire, October 21st
1846, died at Lilleshall, February 27th 1896. M.I. at St.
Michael and All Saints, Lilleshall, Shropshire.

FERGUSON Jno. 14th Regiment of Foot, 40 years, born Tibbermore,
Perth. Admitted to Chelsea Hospital (Chelsea Pensioner)
12/12/1827.

FERGUSON Thomas John, iron merchant of North Leith, age 27
years, son of John Ferguson, deceased. Married by lic. to
Christiana, age 20 years, dau. of Adam POWRIE, bootmaker, at St.
Lukes, Lowton, Lancashire. 17/10/1873.

FERGUSON Margaret, wife of John McINTOSH. See McINTOSH Robert
for details.

FINDLAY Edward born at Arbroath January 1811, died at
Bournemouth February 14th 1876. St. Peter, Bournemouth.

FINDLEY Margaret, wife of George FENWICK, see FENWICK Margaret
for details.

FINDLEY John late of Johnstone, Scotland died 7th September 1849
age 32 years. Elizabeth Turnbull only dau. of above died 17th
August 1861 age 11 years and 1 month. Janet MACFARLANE, his wife
died 1st November 1883 age 67 years. Grave 1565 St. Georges
Churchyard. Castle Street, Liverpool.

FITTIS Mary ann born 1st November 1802, baptised 31st July 1803,
2nd dau. of John Fittis, mariner, native of Dundee, by his wife
Isabella HUMPHREY, native of this parish. St. Hilda's, South
Shields, Co Durham, baptisms.

FLEET Margrett, wife, age 35 years, born Kirkmahoe,
Dumfriesshire, living at Bomear Place, Preston Gubballs,
Shropshire. Husband William, police constable. 1851 census,
Shropshire Rell HO 107/1991 244 030

FLEMING William 65 years, weaver, born Gervin, Scotland. Living
at 175 Spring Gardens, Bolton. With Sarah, wife, 50 years. Emma,
dau, 2 years, both born Bolton. 1851 census Bolton, reel 2211 In
folio 495.

FORBES Richard, unmarried, 20 years, seedsman, born Brechin.
Living at 138 High Street, Toxteth Pk. 1881 census, Toxteth.
Reel RG11/3646, folio 14.

FORDYCE at Gt. Grimsby, Lincs, born Edinburgh, Midlothian. 1881
census, Reel RG11/3267 folio 5.

FORDYCE at Gt. Grimsby, Lincs. born Aberdeenshire. Scotland.
1881 census, reel RG11/3267 folio 5.

FORTIE living at 7 Railway Street, Bolton. Alexander Fortie, 39
years, engineer, born Edinburgh. Christianne, wife, 37 years,
born Ireland, Derry. Alexander, son, 16 years, engineer turner,
born Glasgow. Christian, dau, 12 years, born Glasgow. John, son,
11 years, born Glasgow. Margaret, dau, 3 years, born Bolton.
1861 census, Bolton, reel 6 2832.

FRAZER Rachel, wife of William MAXWELL, see MAXWELL Rachel for
details.

GALLON Rebecca born 18th October 1803, baptised 10th June 1804,
2nd dau. of Thomas Gallon, husbandman, native of Roxburgh, North
Britain, by his wife Ann BAISTER, native of Bolden. St. Hilda's,
South Shields, Co Durham, baptisms.

GATTRICK living at 36 Bengal Square, Bolton, 1851. Robert
Gattrick, 25 years, counterpane weaver, born Bolton. Eliza,
wife, 21 years, bobbin winder, born Edinburgh.

GEDDES Jean, dau. of Jean CROOKSHANK, see CROOKSHANK Jean for
details.

GEDDES Alexander, draper in Liverpool, died 18th October 1847,
age 45 years. William son of John LAURIE, under the Brae,
Dumfries, died 24th May 1848, age 21 years. Alexander son of
Alexander and Elizabeth Geddes (infant). Mary wife of Thomas
LAURIE, draper, Liverpool, died 8th July 1877 age 38 years. St.
James Liverpool, the Necropolis, nonconformists.

GEDDES William of the parish of Leith in the county of
Midlothian in Scotland, bach., and Charlotte TURNER of this
parish, spinster, were married in this church by license, this
28th day Sept. in the year 1809 by me H.W. HUNTER, minister. The
marriage was solemnised between us Wm. Geddes, Charlotte Turner
(both signed) in the presence of Thos. Turner, W. Turner, Maria
Turner, Ellen Turner, Wm. CHAWNER, clerk. Cheadle marriage
register, Staffordshire.

GEE John 43 years, dyer, born Glasgow. Living at 10 Foundry
Street, St. Thomas, Manchester, 1851 census. With Eliz, wife, 38
years, born Manchester, and children Thomas, 15 years, Eliz, 12
years, Sarah, 9 years, Mary, 7 years, John, 3 years, William, 1
year, all born Manchester. Reel 2229 folio152.

GEMMILL John, merchant of Liverpool, formerly of Glasgow, died
6th May 1862, age 74 years. Mary SHARP his wife died 12th May
1853 age 62 years. Their dau. Barbara died 26th May 1842 age 25
years. Janet died 13th December 1853, age 27 years. Eliza
Wilhemina dau. of John and Mary Gemmill and wife of John ROBSON
died 17th January 1866 age 31 years. John son of above John and
Mary died 3rd Sept. 1870 age 49 years. St. James, Liverpool, the
Necropolis, nonconformists.

GEMMELL relict of late Captain William Gemmell of Greenock, died
31st October 1854 age 70 years. An affectionate mother. St.
James, Liverpool.

GIBSON Chas. 15th Regiment of Foot, 36 years, born Dalkeith,
Inverkaling? Midlothian. Admitted to Chelsea Hospital (Chelsea
Pensioner) 4/12/1822.

GIBSON Guy, merchant of Beeth, Scotland, married by license to
Sarah EARDLEY of Leek. 27th February 1776, Horton, Staffordshire

GIBSON Henreietta Anderson, dau of late General Gibson of
Rentland, N.S. died 5th July 1906 aged 56 years, wife of Herbert
W.H. GREEN, vicar of Leamington. M.I. from St. James, Milverton,
Warks.

GILCHRIST Jane, wife of William BROWN, and mother of Jane
BARLOW, see BARLOW Jane for details.

GILCHRIST William, 15th Regiment of Foot, 45 years, born Lo...?
Sutherland. Admitted to Chelsea Hospital (Chelsea Pensioner)
24/10/1821.

GILCHRIST Robert, 15th Regiment of Foot, 31 years, born
Limehouse, Lanark. Admitted to Chelsea Hospital (Chelsea
Pensioner) 26/8/1819.

GILLESPIE Grace, wife of James HILL, see HILL James for details.

GILROY George, 26 years, born Sprouster, Scotland. Living
Northallerton 1851 census. With Mary, wife, 21 years, and Alice,
dau. 3 months old, both born Northallerton, Yorkshire. Reel HO
107/2377 folio 339.

GOLDIE Annabella Frances, died 11th March 1858, 4th daughter of
Thomas Goldie Esq. late of Goldie Leigh in the Stewartry of
Kirkcudbright, Scotland, and Lieu Colonel of 9th Lancers. Also
Charlotte CLARK widow of above, died 29th July 1875 in 87th
year. Also Elizabeth Ann youngest daughter of above deceased at
St. Sepvan, France, 3rd March 1890. M.I. Mont A L'Abbe cemetary,
St. Helier, Jersey, Channel Islands.

GOLDSACK living at St. Margaret at Cliffe, Kent. 1851 census.
George Goldsack, 63 years, mariner, born St. Margarets, Kent.
Margaret, wife, 58 years, born Dundee, Scotland. Reel HO/1632

GOODWIN Margaret, wife of Robert Goodwin, see NEILSON Margaret
for details.

GORDON Alicia, wife of Samuel Gordon and dau. of Alex. McCALLUM,
see McCALLUM Christina for details.

GOWENLOCK John, married, 68 years, coal miner, born Selkirk,
Scotland. 1851 census, Carlisle. Reel Ho 107/2430, folio 217.

GRAHAM Jane, servant, married, 27 years, born Annan, Scotland.
House of John Evans, cotton spinner employing 10 men, 7 boys, 24
women. Grove House, Chipping, Preston. 1851 census.

GRAHAM Jeanie dau. of David Graham of Dumfermline, born 24th
June 1864, died 16th December 1965. M.I. from the Congregational
Chapel, Erdington.

GRAHAM William, 14th Regiment of Foot, 35 years, born
Cannongate, Edinburgh. Admitted to Chelsea Hospital (Chelsea
Pensioner) 4/2/1818.

GRANT Jno. 17th Regiment of Foot, Color Sergant, 39 years, born
....rish? Sutherland. Admitted to Chelsea Hospital (Chelsea
Pensioner) 22/9/1824.

GRAY Alsdr. head, married 40 years, joiner, born Selkirk,
Scotland. Living at Rushen, Isle of Man. 1851 census. With Cath.
wife, 39 years, Andrew, son 4 years, Isa. dau. 2 years,
Christian, dau 10 months, all born Rushen, Isle of Man. Book 2,
page 19, entry 4. From Isle of Man FHS.

GRAY Alexander born 5th June 1802, baptised 25th September 1803,
2nd son of James Gray, mariner, native of Aberdeen, by his wife
Hannah WILBERFORCE, native of this place. St. Hilda's, South
Shields, Co Durham, baptisms.

GRAY John, a Sea Boy, a native of the Island of Westra,
belonging to the ship, "Lord Brougham" of this port, Joseph
Peacock, commander. Aged about 18 years. Burials, Tynemouth,
Christ Church, Northumberland.

GRAY Martha born 17th June 1809, baptised 9th July 1809, 8th
dau. of James Gray, glassmaker, native of Dundee and Ann, his
wife, late HUDSON, native of Alnwick, Northumberland.
Bishopwearmouth, Co Durham, baptisms.

GREEN Henreietta Anderson, dau. of General GIBSON, see GIBSON
Henreietta Anderson for details.

GREENE Margaret, unmarried, 16 years, servant, born Annan,
Scotland. 1851 census Carlisle. Reel HO 107/2430, folio 236.

GRIEG Helen of Leven, Fifeshire, who died on 26th day of March 1852 aged 46 years. St Andrews Parish Church, Ramsbottom.

GREY living at 55 near Blake Hill, Parkstone, Poole area, Dorset. 1851 census. William Grey, head, married, 57 years, farm bailiff, born Northumberland. Frances, wife, 59 years, born Aye, Scotland. Children, Frances, unmarried, 25 years, Robert, 15 years, both born Northumberland.

GRIMSTONE lodging at 56 Every Street, All Souls, Manchester, 1851 census. Eliz. Grimstone, 34 years, unmarried, born Edinburgh. Maria Grimstone, 27 years, schoolteacher, born Edinburgh. House of William and Jessey ROSS. Reel HO 107/2226 page 683.

GUNNING John son of John Gunning, merchant, Annan, died Liverpool 2nd February 1855 age 29 years. Mary BELL relict of above John Gunning, merchant, Annan, died Liverpool 12th February 1857, age 54 years. Janet their dau. died 3rd July 1859 age 19 years. St. James, Liverpool, the Necropolis, nonconformists.

HAIG William, stone mason, native of Berwickshire, Scotland, died 13th March 1842 age 38 years. St. James, Liverpool, the Necropolis, nonconformists.

HAIGH Margaret, dau. of Thomas and Eleanor Haigh of Queensferry, near Edinburgh, servant with Mrs. SHIELDS, Higham Place, died of inflammation in the arm. Aged 25 years. No. 1128 15th January 1835, ward F, No 201, depth 6 feet. Westgate General Cemetary, Elswick, Newcastle upon Tyne.

HALL William, born Kelso 1775 died 21st September 1852 (78). Hannah his wife, born Charlston, South Carolina, 1786, died 5th March 1840 (53). Andrew their son, died 28th May 1838 (2). From "Liverpool Epitaphs" MSS, J. Gibson, Vol. 5. Ancient Chapel, Toxteth Park, (unitarian) Ref. L'pl, record office H929 GIB.

HALLIDAY John formerly of Dumfries, Scotland, died at Liverpool 7th October, 1864 age 45 years. St. James, Liverpool, the Necropolis, noncomformists.

HANNAH living at 155 Butler Street, St Philips, Manchester. 1851 census. David Hannah, 27 years, cotton spinner, born Glasgow. Maria, wife, 30 years, born Chester. Agnes, dau., 6 years, born Manchester. Jessie, dau., 2 years, born Glasgow. James, son, 3 months, born Manchester. Ann APPLETON, mother in law, 46 years, widow, servant, born Chester. Reel HO 107/2226 page 796A.

HANNAH Jessie, late of Newton Stewart, Scotland. Died 26th November 1838 age 27 years. St. James, Liverpool.

HANNAY Captain Robert of Port William, Wigtownshire, died Liverpool 7th December 1838 age 24 years. St. James, Liverpool.

HARDIN Marion, 15 years, pupil at Marine House Ladies Boarding
School, born Agton, Berwickshire. 1861 census, St. Margarets at
Cliffe, Kent.

HARRIS Margaret, 17 years, born Blair Athol, Scotland, servant
in house of John MILLER. 1851 census, Newton by the Sea,
Northumberland. Reel 19 No. 9 Newton coastguard.

HARTLEY William, unmarried, 21 years, farm labourer, born
Glasgow, Scotland. Stokesley union workhouse, 1881 census,
Stokesley, North Riding, Yorkshire.

HATCH living at High Street, Walmer, Kent, 1861 census. John
Hatch, widower, 69 years, retired coastguard officer, born Mddx,
Kensington. Ann Susannah Hatch, dau., unmarried, 34 years, born
Burghed, Scotland.

HAW John, 39 years, journeyman shoemaker, born Glasgow. Living
at 111 Howell Croft, Bolton, 1851 census. With Sarah, wife, 39
years, born Liverpool and children James 12 years, Nanny 11
years, both born Stockport. Rachael 9 years, John 7 years, Alice
5 years, Jane 2 years, all born Bolton. Reel 2211 IM folio 471.

HAY? Margaret, wife of Robert DIXON, see DIXON Margaret for
details.

HAY William, 22 years, unmarried, born Poltney, Caithness,
servant to Henry PEARSON, solicitor. Gr. Blake Street, York.
1851 census.

HEATH Samuel, 40 years, married, engine keeper, born Aberdeen.
Lodging with George THOMAS, light house keeper. South Foreland
Lighthouse. St. Margarets at Cliffe, Kent 1871 census.

HENDERSON wife of Thomas ALDER, see ALDER John for details.

HENDERSON David of Accrington, late of Barlaugh, Ayrshire,
Scotland, who departed this life September 16th 1868 in the
53rd year of his age. Also of Mirron GIRVEN wife of the above
named David Henderson, born at Maybole, Ayrshire January 31st
1815, died at Accrington February 28th 1886. In memory of Robert
eldest son of David and Mirron G. Henderson of Accrington, born
February 3rd 1845 died January 11th 1865. St. Andrew's Parish
Church, Ramsbottom.

HENDERSON George born Dunfermline 6th December 1833, died Boston
25th May 1894, Anna wife Died 22nd February 1896 aged 57 years.
M.I. Boston, Lincs. cemetery.

HENDRY Ann, mother in law of John PORTEUS, see PORTEUS John for
details.

HENRY Elizabeth, born 29th March 1812, baptised 14th April 1812,
2nd dau. of George Henry, labourer, native of Todhurd??, North
Britain, by his wife Christian, dau of William ANDERSON, native
of West Finton or West Sinton?? parish, North Britain. St.
John's, Newcastle upon Tyne, baptisms.

HEPPLESTON living at 11 Albert Terrace, Odo Road, Charlton, Dover. 1871 census. John Heppleston, head, married, 44 years, staff sergeant of militia, born Pontefract, Yorkshire. Mary, wife, 42 years, born Aberdeen. Children, John 15 years, labourer, born Aberdeen. Sarah A. 8 years, born Woolwich, Kent. William J. 6 years, born Shoeburyness, Kent. Walter R. 3 years, born Dover, Kent. Mary E. 5 years, born Dover, Kent. Reel RG 10/1007.

HICKMAN Louisa Helen Gordon, dau. of J.R. COCHRAN. See COCHRAN Louisa Helen Gordon for details.

HILL James wine merchant born Dumfries 29th January 1809, died 10th May 1855 age 46 years. Grace GILLESPIE, his relict died 10th August 1862 age 46 years. George Gill died 25th April, 1863 age 55 years. St. James, Liverpool.

HIRD Elizabeth, dau. of John STEWART, see STEWART Elizabeth for details.

HOOD Elizabeth niece of Margaret Lauder ARMOUR (late of Kilmarnoch, Ayrshire, died 23rd March 1835 age 70 years) and widow of late Alexander Hood, surgeon, Kilmarnock, died 9th August 1856 age 68 years. St. James, Liverpool, the Necropolis, nonconformists.

HORN James, 68 years, tobacconist (journeyman), born Glasgow. Margaret, wife, 64 years, born E. Denhall, Cumb. 97 Union Place, Penrith, 1851 census.

HOWES Sarah, visitor in house of William FAIRBAIRN, see FAIRBAIRN William for details.

HULME living at 136 Spring Gardens, Bolton, 1851 census. Richard Hulme 67 years, dresser of castings at foundry, born Bolton. Isabella wife, 67 years, born Perth, Scotland. Children, Sarah 28 years, cotton reeler, born Butley, Cheshire. Nancy 25 years, cotton reeler. Harriet 22 years, cotton reeler. James 21 years, journeyman tailor. Mirriam 4 years, grand daughter, all born Bolton. Reel 14 2211 In folio 489.

HUNTER Jane Williamson dau. of Andrew Hunter Esq. of Lochrenure, Kirkcudbright, died 15th February 1877 age 61 years. St. James, Liverpool.

HUTCHINSON William, 35 years, born Edinburgh, wife Elizabeth, 35 years, born Penrith. 1851 census, Tirril, Lowther, Cumb.

INNES John, merchant in London, erected a monument to his parents George Innes late Blacksmith in Banff, 1751-1806 and Jane STEWART 1761-1848. M.I. Alvah churchyard, Banffshire.

IRVING Christopher, unmarried, 19 years, clerk, born Kirkcudbright. Lodging at 138 High Street, Toxteth Park. 1881 census, Toxteth. Reel RG11/3646 folio 14.

IRVING David, native of Dumfries died 15th August 1836 (52). From "Liverpool Epitaphs" MSS, J. Gibson, vol. 5 Scotch Church, Rodney Street (presb.) Ref. L'pl record office H929GIB.

JACKSON Ann born 3rd April 1802, baptised 21st November 1802, 1st dau. of Daniel Jackson, bricklayer, native of Stonehive? or Stonehaven? North Britain. St. Hilda's, South Shields, Co Durham, baptisms.

JACKSON Marion, wife of James MILLIGAN, see MILLIGAN James for details.

JAMES John, 28 years, glass blower, born Edinburgh. Living at Oliver Street, Warrington, 1851 census. With Mary, wife 30 years, born Warrington. Benj., son, 1 month, born Warrington.

JAMESON Phillip, 27 years, gas meter marker, born Dundee, Scotland. Living at 14 School Street, Bolton. 1851 census. With Elizabeth, wife, 30 years, born Allbrighton, Shropshire. Margaret Jane, dau., 1 year, born Bolton. Reel 2211 If folio 199a.

JAMIESON Jean, wife of Rev. David Stewart WYLIE, see WYLIE David Stewart for details.

JARVIS James, brother in law of Thomas MOIR, see MOIR Agnes for details.

JOHNSON James, 24 years, lodger, unmarried, piecer in cotton factory, born Annan, Scotland. Living at Spring Gardens, 1851 Bolton, reel 2211 In folio 494.

JOHNSTON Margaret, wife of Adam FAIRRIE, see FAIRRIE Charles Robert for details.

JONES George, senior, 77 years, widower, retired printer, born Aberdeen. Living at 4 Back Verdon Street, Manchester. 1851 census. With George, junior, 51 years, son, printer, born Manchester. Margaret BRYDEN, dau., 39 years, married, born Manchester. George Bryden, 13 years, nephew, born Manchester. Martha Bryden, 12 years, niece, born Manchester. Robert Bryden, 8 years, nephew, born Manchester. Reel 2229.

KAY at Gt. Grimsby, Lincs, born Alyth, Scotland. 1881 census, reel RG11/3267 folio 12.

KERR Andrew, died 24th May 1849 age 58 years. Many years nursery manager of Messrs DICKSON of Hawick, Roxburghshire and latterly with Mr. SKIRVING of Liverpool. Jane his relict of Harsendean Burn, Hawick, died 26th May 1880 age 65 years. Alfred Septimus Kerr, Great Grandson of above, died 12th September 1880 age 6 months. St. James, Liverpool, the Necropolis, nonconformists.

KERR William, head, married, 32 years, tea dealer employing 2 men, born Dumfriesshire, Scotland. Living at 16 West Street, Poole area, Dorset, 1851 census. With Elizabeth, wife, 29 years, born Dorset. Children, Maria, 6 years, born Southampton. George, 5 years, born Wimborne, Dorset. Sarah E., 3 years, born Dorset. John, 3 years, born Dorset. Elizabeth M., 1 year, born Dorset. Archibald BRYDEN, visitor, 34 years, traveller and tea dealer, born Lochmuben, Scotland.

KIELLOR Peter of Perth, Wife Emilia. Children, Bathia, baptised 13/9/1795. James, baptised 8/4/1798, married 1/4/1827, Elizabeth FOTHERINGHAM (b. 12/5/1796, Rhynd, Perth, died 1882 age 85, Islington). Andrew, baptised 4/10/1807, married 28/12/1831, Grace PETERKIN (died 1862 Strand London) died 21/6/1857 age 49 years, Perth, shoemaker. Alexander, birth unknown, married Mary Ann (died 1877 age 68 years, Aston) died 9/1/1882 age 80 years, Islington, grocer. All born Rhynd, Perth.

KIELLOR James, b. 31/10/1828, Leachhill, Perth, son of James and Elizabeth, see KIELLOR Peter.

KIELLOR Mary, b. 12/9/1830, Leachhill, Perth, dau of James and Elizabeth, see KIELLOR Peter. Married Andrew FAIRBAIRN 5/3/1858, Strand, London. Died 1/2/1891 age 60 years. ·

KIELLOR William b. 12/11/1832, Leachhill, Perth, son of James and Elizabeth, see KIELLOR Peter. Married 29/3/1856, Ealing, Jane LACK (b. Hounslow, died 1902 age 66 years Holborn) died 14/3/1916 age 83 years, Holborn, joiner.

KIELLOR John, born 7/5/1835, Leachhill, Perth, son of James and Elizabeth, see KIELLOR Peter. Married 2/10/1861, Balbeggie, Perth, Emily KIELLOR (dau. od Andrew and Grace, b. 18/12/1834, place unknown, see KIELLOR Peter, died 1907 age 73 years, W. Ham) Died 1905 age 70 years, W. Ham. Baker.

KIELLOR Bridget Forsyth, b. 15/8/1837, Leachhill, Perth, dau. of James and Elizabeth, see KIELLOR Peter, married George William BARROW, 16/5/1859, Poplar, London.

KIELLOR Emily, dau of Alexander and Mary Ann, see KIELLOR Peter, married H. J. GALER, no further information.

KINGHORN Geo. married, 34 yrs. Inn keeper, born Moffat, Scotland. 1851 census, Carlisle. Reel HO 107/2430, folio 225.

KNOX Isabella, born 8th July 1804, baptised 5th August 1804, 6th dau. of Thomas KNOX, native of Kelso, North Britain, by his wife Ann NEEL, native of Warkworth. St. Hilda's, South Shields, Co Durham, baptisms.

LAIRD Jennet, wife of John CHISHOLM, see CHISHOLM Jennet for details.

LANG Jane, widow, 55 years, charwoman, born Wick? Scotland. Lodging at 179 Spring Gardens, Bolton. 1851 census, reel 2211 IN, folio 477.

LAURIE Frances, late of Closeburn, Dumfriesshire. No dates. St.
James, Liverpool, the Necropolis, nonconformists.

LAURIE see GEDDES Alexander for details.

LAW Margaret Hope, 4th dau. of James Law Esq. and of Mary his
wife, both of Edinburgh, who died September 16th 18??
(1832,1852,1862?) age 15 years. M>I> Stone No. 089 (5) Headstone
flat and buried. All Saints Church, Epping Upland, Essex. From
Essex Society for family history.

LEARMONTH living at 64 Bradford Road, St Phillips, Manchester,
1851 census. William Learmonth, 42 years, millwright, born
Berwickshire. Jenet, wife, 42 years, born Berwickshire. Children
Margaret, 11 years. Peter, 8 years, both born Manchester. Eliza,
6 years, William, 4 years, both born Berwickshire. Reel
HO107/2226 page 726.

LETHY Andrew, born 3rd January 1808, baptised 16th October 1808,
5th of Andrew Lethy, gardener, native of Eccles, Scotland, and
Christian, his wife, late HUME. Bishopwearmouth, Co Durham,
baptisms.

LEYSHON living at Penarth Hotel, Penarth, Glamorgan, Wales. 1871
census. Thomas Leyshon, head, married, 50 years, railway traffic
supt., born Glamorgan, Cardiff. Jemima, wife, 50 years, born
Edinburgh. Children, Charles, 20 years, clerk. Sarah, 22 years,
both born Pontypridd, Glamorgan. Jenetta, 13 years. Mary, 12
years, both born Victoria, Australia. Margaret, 10 years.
Edward, 9 years, both born Merthyr, Glamorgan. From Glamorgan,
FHS, Cardiff branch.

LITTLE living at 9 Red Bank, Manchester, St. Thomas. 1851
census. John M. Little, 40 years, plumber, glazier, born
Galloway? Jane, wife, 46 years, born Galloway? Children,
Margaret, 10 years, born Salford. James, 7 years. John, 5 years.
Mary Ann, 2 years, all born Manchester. Reel 2229.

LIVINGSTON John (joiner) late of Laurieston, Scotland, died 28th
October 1840 age 27 years. St. James, Liverpool.

LOCK William James, born 6th May 1812, baptised 3rd June 1812,
2nd son of James Lock Esq. native of Edinburgh, by his wife
Agnes, dau. of Joseph LONGSTAFF, native of this chapelry. St.
John's, Newcastle upon Tyne, baptisms.

LOGAN Sarah J., unmarried, 14 years, born Glasgow. Servant in
house of Esther KNOWLES. Back Street, Newchurch, Rossendale.
1861 census.

LOGAN Edward, 30 years, chimney sweep, born Edinburgh. Living at
2 Back Ridgefield, Manchester, St Ann. 1851 census. With Betsey,
wife, born Salford. Children, Robert, 8 years. Frances, 3 years.
Ann, 8 months. All born Salford. Also John MORRIS, 18 years,
son!, and Wm. 16 years? son! both born Manchester. Reel 2229.

LOGAN John son of late Dr. Logan, Maybole, Scotland. Died 15th
April 1843 age 29 years. St. James, Liverpool.

LOW William, unmarried, 25 years, rail guard, born Booth,
Ayrshire. 1851 census, Carlisle. Reel HO 107/2430, folio 452.

LUTET Mary Oaten, born April 14th 1803, baptised 24th December
1803, 1st dau. of John Lutet, mariner, native of Stromness,
North Britain, by his wife, Elizabeth OATEN, native of
Sunderland. St. Hilda's, South Shields, Co Durham, baptisms.

LYMBURN Andrew, merchant, native of Paisley, died 23rd July 1837
(41). From "Liverpool Epitaphs" MSS, J. Gibson, vol. 5 Scotch
Church, Rodney Street, (presb.) Ref. L'pl record office H929
GIB.

MAIR William, born 19th February 1809, baptised 19th March 1809,
2nd son of Alexander MAIR, weaver of Glasgow, and Sarah, his
wife, late TENANT?, native of this parish. Bishopwearmouth, Co
Durham, baptisms.

MALLARD Robert, 38 years, cotton spinner, born Glasgow. Living
at 40 William Street, Ancoats. 1881 census. With Mary, wife, 37
years, born Manchester. Children, John, 14 years. George, 11
years. Sarah, 8 years. All born Manchester. Reel 2855 Dist. 17.

MARR James, 15th Regiment of Foot, 37 years, born Fraserburgh.
Admitted to Chelsea Hospital (Chelsea pensioner) 2/2/1820.

MARTIN Thomas, formerly of Dundee, died 8th September 1837 (34).
From "Liverpool Epitaphs" MSS, J. Gibson, vol. 5, Scotch Church,
Rodney Street, (presb.) Ref. L'pl record office H929 GIB.

MARTIN William, husband of Janet WANNAN, see WANNAN Janet for
details.

MATHESON James, native of Dundee, died 6th December 1844 (40)
From "Liverpool Epitaphs" MSS, J. Gibson, vol. 5, Scotch Church,
Rodney Street, (presb.) Ref. L'pl record office H929 GIB.

MATHEWS living at 22 Holland Street, Manchester, All Souls, 1851
census. James Mathews, 44 years, hammerman, born Scotland.
Margaret, wife, 38 years, born Edinburgh. Janet, dau., 10 years,
born Dundee. Mary CATTO, 26 years, unmarried, relation, born
Dalkeith. Reel HO 107/2226 page 687/687A.

MATHEWS Peter, married, 48 years, licenced victualler, born
Lochee, Forfarshire. Living at Bell Inn, Church Road, Holborne,
Staffordshire. 1851 census.

MAUN? Alexander, artist, born Glasgow, 22/1/1853, died Streatham
26/1/1908. M.I. Blewbury, Berks.

MAUN Hannah, 30 years, wife, born Glasslees, Wigtonshire. Living
at 40 Aldermanbury, London. 1851 census.

MAXWELL Rachel wife of William Maxwell of Liverpool and 2nd dau.
of late Alexander FRAZER of Frazerfield, Aberdeenshire, died
13th February 1867 in 67th year. William Maxwell died 17th
November 1869 age 78 years. James Maxwell their son born 31st
October 1833, died 7th September 1881. St. James, Liverpool.

MAXWELL Francis, formerly of Drumpark, Kirkcudbrightshire, died
29th May 1876 age 68 years. Thomas his only son died 13th May
1855 age 20 years. Jane his eldest dau., died 17th August 1872
age 32 years at Leamington, Warwickshire. St. James, Liverpool.

MAXWELL Margaret, wife of George Maxwell, died Liverpool 7th May
1837 age 31 years. Clark 4th son died Liverpool 28th April 1839
age 11 years. George Maxwell died Liverpool 11th February 1858
age 62 years. Alexander 4th Child of Wellwood and Elizabeth
Maxwell died Liverpool 22nd April 1863 age 16 months. Wellwood
Maxwell died at Glenlee 12th July 1866 age 36 years. Buried
Churchyard of Kells, Kirkcudbright. Elizabeth 3rd child of above
died Liverpool 6th May 1871 age 11 years. St. James, Liverpool.

MAXWELL Thomas 2nd son of George and Margaret Maxwell died at
Dumfries 28th July 1833 age 17 months. Interred in Barncleugh
ground, St. Michaels, Dumfries. George Maxwell 3rd son drowned
in River Ken, Kirkcudbright 21st September 1854, buried same
place. St. James, Liverpool.

MAY Thomas, born 22/1/1900, Edinburgh, died November 1986,
Mansfield, son of Samuel and Jessie (BROWN) May. U.S.A.
obituaries, Sun Chronicle, Rhode Island.

MEARNS John born 29th May 1810, baptised 24th June 1810, 2nd son
of John MEARNS, carpenter, native of Aberdeenshire and
Elizabeth, his wife, late FORSTER, native of Bebside,
Northumberland. Bishopwearmouth, Co Durham, baptisms. See next
entry.

MEARNS Thomas born 28th June 1808, baptised 31st July 1808, 1st
son of John Mearns, carpenter, native of Old Macca, Aberdeen and
Elizabeth, his wife, native of Bebside, Northumberland. See
previous entry. Bishopwearmouth, Co Durham, baptisms.

MEARNS Captain William, son of Captain Andrew Mearns of
Montrose, Scotland, died 21st August 1815 age 34 years. Grave
157, St. Georges Churchyard, Castle Street, Liverpool.

MELLOR or MELLON living at 6 Gerrards Court, Ancoats, 1881
census. Bridget, head, married, 32 years, charwoman, born
Glasgow. Children Catherine, 10 years. Anne, 7 years. Susan, 3
years, all born Glasgow. Reel 2855, Dist. 10.

MIDDLETON Mary, dau. of H. ROSS, for many years coachman to the
Duke of Buccleugh, died 20th May 1855 age 50 years. St. James,
Liverpool.

MILLER Matthew, of Liverpool, son of Rev. Dr. Miller of Cumnock,
Ayrshire. Died 14th March 1833 age 46 years. St. James,
Liverpool.

MILLER living at Newton by the Sea, Northumberland. 1851 census.
John Miller, head, 48 years, chief officer, born Edinburgh. M??,
wife, 38 years, born Fife. Scotland. Children, Arch. D. 12
years, born Vanliemans Land. Andrew, 10 years, Born Mid.
Portobello. John, 7 years, born Vandeman Land. Rachael, 3 years,
born Fife , St. Andrews. Reel 19 No. 9 Newton Coastguard.

MILLIGAN James of Liverpool, merchant, born at Dumfries 30th
April 1764, died in London 1st April 1826. Marion his wife,
eldest Dau. of Robert JACKSON Esq. Provost at Dumfries, born
Edinburgh 7th August 1766 died Liverpool 7th February 1826. From
"Liverpool Epitaphs" MSS, J. Gibson vol. 5. Scotch Church,
Oldham Street, (presb.) Ref. L'pl record office H929 GIB.

MILNE James, minister at Sandwich, Kent. Eldest son of George
Milne, of Greenlaw (1702-1772) and Isobel MONRO. M.I. Alvah,
Banffshire.

MITCHELL George Douglas of Kirkcaldy. Rusholm Road, Cemetery.
(now belongs to William Mitchell, writer, Kirkcaldy).

MOFFATT at Cliffe House Boy's Boarding School. 1871 census, St
Margarets at Cliffe, Kent. Frederick Moffatt, 9 years, pupil
boarder, born Edinburgh. Tom. H. Moffatt, 7 years, pupil
boarder, born Edinburgh.

MOFFITT living at 33 Buxton Street, Newcastle-upon-Tyne, East
All Saints. 1871 census. Roger? Moffitt, head, married, 37
years, house painter, born Berwick, Scotland. Jane, wife, 28
years, born Berwick, Scotland.

MOIR Agnes, native of Falkirk, Stirlingshire, Scotland, died 2nd
July 1860 (1866?) no age given. Thomas Moir died 6th November
1867. Catherine Moir, sister died 21st June 1873. James JARVIS,
brother in law of above, died 3rd July 1887 age 63 years. Jessie
Moir wife of James Jarvis died 8th October 1888. Interred
Falkirk cemetery. Grave 1900 St. Georges Churchyard, Castle
street, Liverpool.

MONGTON Alfred, unmarried, 24 years, boarder, med. assistant,
born alloa. Living with William G. FORBES, G.P. born Scotland.
1881 census, Stockesley, North riding Yorkshire.

MONRO Isobel wife of George MILNE, see MILNE James for details.

MONTGOMERY James born 1771, Halfway, Irvine, son of a Moravian
missionary. Left Irvine c1776 for N. Ireland, died Sheffield
1854, journalist, hymn writer, poet and lecturer.

MOORE Ann, unmarried, 17 years, born Louth, Dundalk. general
servant in house of John F. RICHARDSON. 102 New Street,
Birmingham, St. Philip. 1851 census, En 14, sch23, page 441.

MOORE Margaret wife of Arthur Moore, merchant of Liverpool and
dau. of Adam and Margaret FAIRRIE (see FAIRRIE Charles Robert)
late of Greenock, died 25th Aug. 1865 age 34. Buried here. Percy
their son died 22nd Feb. 1866 age 10 mths. St. James Liverpool

MORGAN Jane, wife of David SINCLAIR, see SINCLAIR Joseph for details.

MORICE Hercules, a native of Benholm in Co Kincardine, died 23rd February 1844 age 68 years. A confidential and faithful clerk in the stamp office, Liverpool for nearly 18 years. St. James, Liverpool, the Necropolis, nonconformists.

MORRISON Elizabeth, 20 years, born Gallowayshire. 1851 census, Northallerton. Reel HO 107/2377 folio 342.

MOSE Agnes, late of Broughty Ferry, Dundee, died 23rd November 1861 age 61 years. Grave 157B, St. Georges Churchyard, Castle Street, Liverpool.

MOSTYN living at Boundary Road, Eccleston, St. Helens. 1851 census. George Mostyn, head, 42 years, Curate St. Thomas, born Sligo. Charlotte, wife, 32 years, born Glasgow, Scotland. Children, William, 8 years. Mary, 6 years, both born Glasgow. Emily, 5 years, born Blackburn, lancs. Louisa, 4 years, born St. Helens, Lancs.

MOW Elizabeth, born 12th December 1806, baptised 3rd May 1810, 2nd dau. of John Mow, glassman, native of Alloa, Scotland and Barbara, his wife, late TAYLOR, native of this parish. Bishopwearmouth, co Durham, baptisms.

MOWAT Alex of Wick, mariner, married Mary KNOWLES with consent of father, by license. 5/2/1836 Walton on the Hill.

MOWAT Joyse born 13th December 1803, baptised 29th January 1804, 2nd dau. of James Mowat, mariner, native of Orkney, North Britain, by his wife Joyce ATKINSON, native of Sunderland. St. Hilda's, South Shields, Co Durham, baptisms.

MUIR Jane, wife of James DREW, see DREW Jane for details.

MUIR Janet, (nee THOMPSON) relict of John Muir Esq. of Peel Thornton, Lanarkshire. Died 9th April 1844 age 73 years. Mary youngest dau. of above died 10th March 1872. Margaret, 2nd dau. of above, died 28th August 1881 age 76 years. St. James, Liverpool, the Necropolis, nonconformists.

MUNRO In loving memory of John Munro, farmer, Berrylane, who died January 12th 1906 aged 74 years. Also his dau. Georgina who died at Manchester on May 8th 1917 aged 35 years. Also Georgina LEDINGHAM, wife of the above John Munro, died at clayfolds, Alvah, December 29th 1926 age 83 years. Fordyce Parish Church, Banffshire.

MURE John, merchant, native of Kirkcudbrightshire, died 10th August 1853 (73). From "Liverpool Epitaphs" MSS, J. Gibson, vol. 5 Scotch Church, Oldham Street, (presb.) Ref. L'pl record office H929 GIB.

MURDOCH Thomas of Liverpool, native of Ayrshire, Scotland, died
21st June 1835 age 44 years, husband of Margaret. Infant son,
John died 14th February 1832 age 6 months. St. James, Liverpool.

MURRAY Donald, a native of Dornoch, North Scotland who departed
this life January 2nd 1865 in the 81st of his age. Also of
Margaret Murray the wife of Donald Murray a native of Dornoch,
who departed this life July 30th 1845 age 56 years. Also of
William Murray son of the above who departed this life December
31st 1884 age 69 years. Also of Betsy his wife who departed this
life June 25th 1888 age 71 years. St. Andrews Parish Church,
Ramsbottom.

MURRAY William of Roundburnhead, North Britain, a traveller.
Buried 8th September 1781. Ovingham, Northumberland, burials.

MYLNE Helena Joan Weatherall, wife of Edmund PERCY, see PERCY
Helena Joan Weatherall for details.

MYLNE William Craig, born Glasgow November 1805, died Liverpool
22nd October 1855. St. James, Liverpool.

MYRTLE William, born Edinburgh 1sr August 1812, died at
Parkfield Road, Liverpool, 8th April 1877. Toxteth Cemetery,
Smithdown Road, Liverpool.

McANDREW Mary relict of James McAndrew of Elgin, Scotland, born
Lisbon 12th December 1764, died Liverpool 7th April 1848 age 83
years. St. James, Liverpool.

McBRYDE James, 40 years, born Gallowayshire. 1851 census
Northallerton, rell HO 107/2377 folio 342.

McCALLUM Christina, wife of late Alexander McCallum of
Argyleshire, died 22nd January 1857 age 76 years. Nancy their
2nd dau. died 20th October 1862 age 55 years. Alicia widow of
Samuel GORDON and 4th dau. of above died 16th February 1869 age
52 years. St. James, Liverpool, the Necropolis, nonconformists.

McCALLUM Margaret, widow, 54 years, servant domestic, born
Perthshire. 1881 census, Stokesley, North Riding of Yorkshire.

McCONNOCHIE Robert (junior), Clarence Foundary, Liverpool, late
of Glenluce, Scotland, died December 16th 1839 age 46 years.
Errected by his brother David McConnochie. St. James, Liverpool.

McCORMICK John, head, married, 40 years, boot hodder, born
Gallaway, Scotland. Living at 166 Love Lane, Poole area, Dorset.
1851 census. With Maria, wife, 34 years, born Purbeck, Dorset.
Children, Henry Stickland, 5 years. Maria, 3 days, both born
Purbeck, Dorset. Reel HO 107.

MACDERMID James of Liverpool, formerly of Glasgow, died 9th May
1857 age 52 years. Alexander his son, died July 1852, 14 years.
St. James, Liverpool.

MACDONALD Ann - Mrs. born 1897 St. Combs, Aberdeenshire, died
November 1986, Foxboro. Dau. of William and Annie (BRUCE) COW.
Graduated Fraserburgh High school and Bradford, England. U.S.A.
obituaries, Sun Chronical, Rhode Island.

McDONALD Donald, 27 years, cashire at chemical works, born
Invernesshire. 1851 census, Taskers Road, Kiersley. Reel 2206 Ib
folio 42a.

MACDONALD John Angus, born Fort William 1893 died 11th May 1962,
and wife Janet, died 1941 and was buried at Hawkeshead Cemetery,
Paisley. M.I. from Church of the Resurrection, Hurley and Wood
End, Warks.

McDOWALL John a native of Wigtownshire, Scotland. Died 31st July
1833 age 28 years. Also by a bereaved mother to the memory of an
only son James PORTER M.D. a native of Greenock. Died suddenly
1st August 1833 age 23 years. St. James, Liverpool, the
Necropolis, nonconformists.

McFARLANE Catherine More, born 2nd December 1805, baptised 1st
January 1809, 2nd dau. of Archibald More McFarlane, shoemaker,
native of Down, Perthshire and Mary, his wife, late WILKINSON,
native of Monkwearmouth. Bishopwearmouth, Co Durham, baptisms.

MACFARLANE Janet, wife of John FINDLEY, see FINDLEY John for
details.

McGILL David, born St. Johns, Dalry, Kirkcudbrightshire,
Scotland, died Victoria Terrace, Dudley 21st September 1864 age
55 years. M.I. from King Street Independent Chapel, Dudley.

McGILL Peter of Oakmere, formerly of Nether Carrell, Kirkmichael
Dumfries, died 20th March 1869 age 51 years. M.I. Delamere
Church.

McGREGOR Hugh, 46 years, born Glasgow. 1851 census,
Northallerton. With Sarah, wife, 38 years, born Witchbole, Wor.
Children, John, 12 years, born Soho, Mdx. Harriet, 10 years.
Hugh, 8 years. Sarah, 7 years, all born Plaistow, Ess. Robert, 2
years. William 11 months. Both born Northallerton, Yorkshire.
Reel HO 107/2377 folio 382.

McGREGOR James, unmarried, 27 years, under butler at Manor
House, born Perth. 1851 census, Stokesley, North Riding,
Yorkshire.

McGREGOR living at 4 Wood Street, Bedford, Lancs. 1871 census.
Robert McGregor, 32 years, reaping machine fitter, born Keith,
Scotland. Ann, wife, 21 years, born Keith. Ann J. 3 years, dau.
born Keith. Alex. 1 year, son, born Grantham, Lincs.

McINTOSH Robert, born 6th Sept. 1811, baptised 25th Dec. 1811,
7th son of John McIntosh, glassmaker, native of Bolrophay
Parish, North Britain, by his wife Margaret, dau. of Andrew
FERGUSON, native of Kelso Parish, Roxburgh. St. Johns, Newcastle
upon Tyne, baptisms.

McKAY living at 181 Chorley New Road, Bolton, 1871 census. Ann
McKay, 22 years, domestic housemaid, born Dysart, Fifeshire.
Mary McKay, 18 years, domestic nurse, born Edinburgh. Reel 8
3936.

McKELVIE James, cook of the brig "Albion" of Dundee, Captain
David KIDD, died at the house of Matthew CROOKS, Bull Ring. Age
27 years. 13th April 1838?. Tynemouth, Christ Church,
Northumberland, burials.

MACKENY Barbara, servant, unmarried, 32 years, born Orkney Isle.
1851 census, 3 St. Johns Place, Christchurch, Marylebone, Mdx.
Reel HO 107/1490.

McLEAN, Mary, native of Girvan, Ayrshire, Scotland, spouse of
Andrew PEACOCK, born 11th October 1809, died 24th February 1856.
Helen dau. of above, born 10th March 1841, died 23rd February
1861. Above Andrew Peacock, born 16th July 1808, died 14th
September 1863. Grave 1947 St. Georges Churchyard, Castle
Street, Liverpool.

McLEOD Margaret A. married, 63 years, born Argyll. 138 High
Street, Toxteth Park, Toxteth. 1881 census. Reel RG11/3646 folio
14.

MACLOUD Mary, wife of John TEMPLEMAN, see TEMPLEMAN John for
details.

McMILLAN Duncan, carter, Townhead, Irving. Attended Baptist
Church. 2 sons Daniel born Arran 1813. Alexander born 1818.
Daniel moved to Stirling, the Glasgow as a bookseller. Alexander
was a schoolteacher in Irvine, the Glasgow. Both moved to London
and ran a bookshop in Aldergate Street, from which sprang the
publishing firm.

McMINN, merchant of Crossmichael, Galloway, came to liverpool
1796, died 26th February 1855 in 76th year. St. James,
Liverpool.

MACNICOL Mary Anabella, born Edinburgh 29th March 1806, died
23rd September 1886. M.I. from St. Mary Magdalene, Lillington,
Wks.

MACQUEEN Archibald, M.D., born Arrondale?, Scotland, 1849, died
in Market Drayton, 1938. M.I. 14 St. Mary's Churchyard, Market
Drayton, Shropshire.

McWILLIE living at Leyburn, Yorkshire, 1881 census. John
McWillie, 35 years, road surveyer, highways, born Banffshire.
Ann, wife, 30 years, born Banffshire. Children, Ann Scott, 11
years. Mary, 8 years. Jane, 6 years, all born Perth. John, 2
years, born Carperby, Yorkshire. Ellen, 3 months, born Leyburn,
Yorkshire.

NAPPIER John born 9th Jan. 1803, bapt. 6th Feb. 1803, 1st son of
James Nappier, mariner, native of Arbroath, North Scotland, by
his wife Isabella BEST of Durham. St. Hilda, South Shields.

NEILSON Margaret, of Glasgow in North Britain married Robert
GOODWIN of this parish, surgeon, 15th September 1827, both
signed, witnesses, John MINSHALL, Anne NEILSON. Over St. Chad,
Cheshire.

NELSON Jane, wife of James PATTISON, see PATTISON John Nelson
for details.

NEVILL Isabella, 14 years, born Glasgow, pupil boarder at Marine
House Ladies Boarding School, St. Margaret's at Cliffe, Kent.
1871 census.

NIEL Peter C., unmarried, 23 years, born Perthshire. Lodger in
household of John BUDDEN, 30 Oakley Street, Poole area, Dorset.
1851 census.

NEILL Robert, 29 years, china dealer and repairer, born Glasgow.
Living at 6 Stonegate, St. Helen's , Yorkshire. 1851 census.
With Cath., wife 37 years, born Kildare Ireland. Children, John,
9 years, born Bristol. Joseph, 7 years, born Malmesbury, Wilts.

NICOL living at Gulborn Street, Warrington. 1851 census. Edward
Nicol, 53 years, ships carpenter, born Tarbolon? or Tarbolton?
Cath. wife, 52 years, children, Barbara, 22 years, Edward, 14
years, all born Dumbarton.

OGILVY Marcia A. S., sister in law of Thomas H. YORKE, see YORKE
for details.

ORR living at Leadbeter Fold, Little Lever, Bolton. 1851 census.
John Orr, 43 years, plasterer, born Edinburgh. Margaret, wife,
42 years, born Hawick, Scotland. Children, Catriana, 20 years,
servant, born Glasgow. Henry, 18 years, born Glasgow. William,
14 years, joiner. Andrew, 14 years, labourer. Isabel, 11 years,
all born Hawick, Scotland. John, 9 years, born Cumberland. Reel
2211 2Db folio 640a.

PANTON Thomas William, born 22nd October 1807, baptised 23rd
October 1808, 1st son of Hugh Panton, grocer, native of Alyth,
Perthshire, and Elizabeth, his wife, late PUNSHOW, native of
Sunderland. Bishopwearmouth, Co Durham, baptisms.

PARKER Alexander, head, 49 years, farmer 35 acres, born
Glasserton, Kirkcudbright, Scotland. Living at 82 Strawberry
Hill, Longfleet, Poole area, Dorset. 1851 census. With Mary,
wife, 46 years, born Wighton Shore, Dorset. Children, John, 16
years, attorneys clerk. Andrew, 11 years. Jennet, 9 years.
Alexander, 8 years. Margaret, 6 years. All born Longfleet,
Dorset. Reel HO 107.

PATTERSON John, 26 years, married, engine fitter, born Greenock.
Lodger in house of Roger GREEN, 95a Shuttle Street, Atherton.
1871 census.

PATTISON John Nelson, born 10th February, baptised 27th March
1808, 3rd son of James Pattison, ships carpenter, native of
Hawthorn? and Jane his wife, late NELSON, native of St. Ingans,
Scotland. Bishopwearmouth, Co Durham, baptisms.

PATTISON Margaret, born 26th November 1802, baptised 26th June
1808, 1st dau. of James Pattison, mariner, decd., native of
Arbroath, Scotland, and Mary, his wife, late ASHTON, native of
Helmsley, Yorkshire. Bishopwearmouth, Co Durham, baptisms.

PEACOCK Andrew, husband of Mary McLEAN, see McLEAN Mary for
details.

PERCY Helena Joan Weatherall, wife of Edmund PERCY, dau. of
William MYLNE of Lockhill, East Lothian, born 21st February
1858, died 13th July 1918. M.I. St. Peter's, Worfield, Shrops.

PHILLIPS Margaret, born 3rd December 1803, baptised 30th
September 1804, 3rd dau. of John Phillips, mariner, native of
Aberdeen, by his wife Catherine DOBBINSON, native of this place.
St. Hilda's, South Shields, Co Durham, baptisms.

PINKERTON living at Smith View, Whitfield, Glossop, Derbyshire.
1851 census. David Pinkerton, 35 years, calico printer, born
Glasgow. Alice, wife, 31 years, born Kirk Lanes, Lancs.
Children, Mary Jane, 8 years, born Edinburgh. James Henry, 6
years. Ellen, 4 years. Eliza Ann, 1 year, all born Whitfield,
Derbyshire.

POLLOCK living at Darenth, Kent. 1851 census. Alexander Pollock,
47 years, born Edinburgh. Jane, wife, 45 years, born Aberdeen.
Elizabeth, dau., 23 years, born Edinburgh. Reel 1607, page 26.

POLLOCK John born 23rd March 1804, baptised 30th December 1804,
4th son of Andrew Pollock, bottlemaker, native of Glasgow, by
his wife Margaret SHOLTON or SHOTTON, native of Lyth. St.
Hilda's, South Shields, baptisms.

PORTEUS Barbara Ann born 29th October 1802, baptised 31st
October 1803, 1st dau. of Henry Porteus, mariner of East
Louthier, by his wife Elizabeth ROBSON, native of this place.
St. Hilda's, South Shields, Co Durham, baptisms.

PORTEOUS living at Punch Bowl, Mewith, Bentham, Yorkshire. 1881
census. John Porteous, head, widow, 56 years, surveyor or
Chelsea Pensioner? born Midlothian, Scotland. Children, Jane,
unmarried, 29 years, Col. Sergt. Royal Eng. clerk in office,
born Castleton, Yorkshire. Margaret, unmarried, 26 years, Inn
Keepers dau. born Ayr, Scotland. Mary, unmarried, 24 years,
dress maker, born Ayr. Agnes, unmarried, 20 years, Inn Keepers
dau. born Southampton, Hants. Reel RG11/4297, folio 29.

PORTEUS living at Ancroft mains, Northumberland. 1851 census.
John, married, 53 years, agr. worker, Eliz. H., wife 53 years,
both born Lowick, Scotland. Children, James, 25 years, born
Berrington. George, 23 years, Eliz. H. 21 years, both born
Lowick. Ann HENDRY, mother in law, widow, 79 years, born

Learmouth. Reel 20. 1851 census.

PORTER James, mariner of Arbroath, Scotland, died of Cholera. No. 395, 1st Aug. 1832, ward x, No. 134, age 21 years. Newgate Cemetery, Elswick, Newcastle-u-Tyne, Interments.

PORTER James M.D. see McDOWALL John for details.

POTTS Alexander, 50 years, sawyer, born Glasgow. Living at 105 Spring Gardens, Bolton. With Betty, wife, 50 years, born Manchester. Children, Jane, 17 years. Joseph, 13 years. James, 8 years. Sarah, 6 years. Betty, 3 years, all born Bolton. 1851 census, reel 2211 IL folio 411.

PROCTOR Elizabeth, wife of Charles SMITHERN, see SMITHERN Alfred Henry for details.

PUNSHOW Sarah, born 26th April 1808, baptised 18th October 1808, 2nd dau. of Richard Punshow, mason, native of this parish and Ann, his wife, late WILSON, native of Edinburgh. Bishopwearmouth, Co Durham, baptisms.

PURVES Margaret, wife of Thomas THOMPSON, see THOMPSON James for details.

QUINET Alexander, late of Portabello, Edinburgh, died 14th June 1849, age 37 years. M.I. from All Saints, Leamington Spa, Warks.

RAGAN Margaret, unmarried, 28 years, house servant and cook, born Scotland, near Edinburgh. Lived with Dr. William John Strother and family. 1851 census, Stokesley, North Riding Yorkshire.

RAILTON Rev. Lancelot, born at Barnard Castle 23rd June 1811, died at Peel, November 9th 1864. Margaret Railton, born at Edinburgh, October 10th 1814, died at Peel, November 10th 1864. Source: Peel Wesleyan Chapel, Peel, Isle of Man. From Isle of Man FHS.

REDHEAD living at Great Moor Street, Bolton. Thomas Warrinor Redhead, 44 years, victualler, born Cartmell, Lancs. Mary Wood Redhead, wife 36 years, born Galway, Scotland. Children, Thomas Warrinor, 5 years. William Warrinor, 9 years. Alexander Warrinor, 3 years. Arthur Warrinor, 11 months, all born Bolton. John, father, 70 years, born Milnthorpe, Westmoreland. Elizabeth, mother, 68 years, born Cartmell, Lancs. 1851 census, reel 2211 IL folio 391.

REDPATH James, born 7th? January 1809, baptised, 28th May 1809, 4th son of William Redpath, labourer, native of Dunce, Scotland, and Ann his wife, late WATSON, native of this parish. Bishopwearmouth, Co Durham, baptisms.

REED William, born 7th June 1803, bapt. 21st Aug. 1803, 3rd son of John Reed, flaxdresser, native of Perth, North Britain, by his wife Jennet HUGET native of Morrick, Northumberland. St. Hilda's, South Shields, Co Durham, baptisms.

REID Catherine Stalkhouse, wife of W.D. Reid, late of
Ellenreich, North Britain, died Milverton 3rd July 1869, age 78
years. M.I. St. James, Milverton, Warks.

REID Thomas, 27 years, engineer, born Dundee, Luchie? or Sackie?
Living at 16 Spring Gardens, Bolton. With Charlotte, wife, 30
years. Children, William, 5 years. Mary Jane, 2 years, all born
Bolton. 1851 census, reel 2211 In folio 478.

RIDDELL Henry, 37 years, letterpress printer, born Glasgow.
Living at 1 Ridgefield, Manchester, St. Ann's. 1851 census. With
Ann, wife, 33 years, eating house keeper, born Horbury,
Yorkshire. Reel 2229.

RIDDLE James, late of Kintore, Aberdeenshire, died (at the Ford)
Clanmartin. May 11th 1903 age 60 years. M.I. Langstone Parish
Church, Gwent. ⟍

RIGG James, 49 years, machine turner, born Paisley, Scotland.
Living at Barn Street, Bolton. 1851 census. With Eleanor, wife,
47 years, born Llanrwist, Denbighshire. William, son, 8 years,
born Bolton. Reel 2211 Ic folio 514a.

ROAN James, native of Dumfries, Scotland, died 3rd August 1848
age 46 years. Leonard Smith Roan his son, died 14th February
1861 age 23 years, at Thornhill, Wavertree, Liverpool. David
Roan son of above, died at Hamilton C.W. 14th April 1868 age 33
years. Francis Roan son of above, died at the Priory, Childwell,
Liverpool. St. James, Liverpool, the Necropolis, nonconformists.

ROBB Islay C. 57 years, law writer, born Glasgow. Living at 15
Tasle alley, Manchester, St. Ann, 1851 census. With Eliza, wife,
59 years, born Manchester. James, son, 16 years, born Liverpool.
Reel 2229.

ROBERTS Edward, 21 years, glass blower, born Glasgow. Living at
Orford Lane, Warrington. 1851 census. With Susana, wife, 21
years, born Manchester. John, son, 1 year, born Manchester.

ROBERTSON at Grimsby, Lincs. 1881 census, born Glasgow. Reel
RG11/3267 folio20.

ROBERTSON Jean, wife of William ELLIOT, see ELLIOT William, M.D.
for details.

ROBERTSON Margaret, born 12th February 1804, baptised 10th March
1805, 2nd dau. of Thomas ROBERTSON, mariner, native of
Stromness, by his wife Elizabeth KIRKTON, native of this parish.
St. Hilda's, South Shields, Co Durham, baptisms.

ROBINSON Ann Jane, 30 yrs, unmarried, washer, born Glasgow.
Lodging at 5 Pump Houses, Bolton, with Robert Robinson, 13 yrs,
weaver, born Manchester. 1851 census, reel 2211 Ie folio 153.

ROBSON Eliza Wilhemina, dau. of John GEMMILL, see GEMMILL John
for details.

ROME Andrew, 22 years, unmarried, born Gretna. Lodger with William Hill, 20 Russell Street, All Souls, Manchester. 1851 census.

ROSEBERRY William, born 10th February, baptised 12th July 1807, 1st son of Peter Roseberry, mason, native of A??ton Ford, Scotland (crease at ??) and Jane his wife, late BRECKENBRIDGE, native of Monkwearmouth. Bishopwearmouth, Co Durham, baptisms.

ROSS erected by David and Agnes Ross of Maybole, Ayrshire, Scotland. In memory of their son John who died at Seddon's farm, Elton, on 20th July 1861 age 26 years. Also of Margaret their dau. who died at Milton, Ayrshire on 28th of April 1848 age 13 years. Also of David Ross who died at Old Hall Farm, Pilkington, May 22nd 1875 age 31 years. Also of David Ross, senior, who died at Stand Cottage May 22nd 1883 aged 71 years. Also of Oliver their son, who died January 30th 1885 aged 42 years. Also of Agnes wife of David Ross, senior, who died April 24th 1887 aged 76 years. St. Andrews Parish Church, Ramsbottom.

ROSS Mary Ann, born 24th June 1807, baptised 6th January 1808, 1st dau. of John Ross, a soldier in the Royal Artillery, native of Forfar, Angleshire and Mary, his wife, late WATSON, native of Offerton. Bishopwearmouth, Co Durham, baptisms.

ROY James, Lieut and Qtr. Master, late of Aberdeenshire Militia, died at residence of his son in law Mr. James COCKER, 5th May 1850 age 76 years. Also infant son , Godfrey, of James and Margaret Cocker, died 18th May 1851, 1 month. St. James, Liverpool, the Necropolis, nonconformists.

RUSSELL James, 42 years, weaver, born Glasgow. Living at 5 Bengal Square, Bolton. With Nancy, wife, 26 years, bobbin winder. Francis, son, 4 years, both born Bolton, and Corbatt MOFFAT, 42 years, lodger, weaver, born Scotland. 1851 census, reel 2211 Ig folio 214.

RUSSELL Jessie, age 34 years, unmarried, cook, born Stirling, Scotland. 1881 census, Guestling, Sussex.

SANDS John, merchant of Liverpool, son of the late Rev. James Sands, minister of Lerwick, died 2nd June 1840, age 54 years. Erected by a few friends. St. James, Liverpool.

SANGSTER William Bruce, son of Barbara BRUCE, see BRUCE Barbara for details.

SANGSTER Alexander, ship master, Saltcoats, Ayrshire. Died 17th January 1827 (35). From "Liverpool Epitaphs" MSS, J. Gibson, vol. 5 Scotch Church, Rodney Street, (presb.) Ref. L'pl record office H929 GIB.

SCOLLAY John born 21st January 1805, baptised 14th April 1805, 5th son of John Scollay, mariner, native of Lorwick, Shetland, by his wife, Elizabeth GATES, native of this place. St. Hilda's, South Shields, Co Durham, baptisms.

SCOTT living at Cinnamon Brow, Warrington. 1851 census. John Scott, 27 years, corn miller, (employ 3 men), born Dumfries. Mary, wife 23 years, born Winwick. James, 21 years, brother, born Scotland. Ann Smith, 12 years, niece, born Liverpool. John Smith, 4 years, nephew, born Liverpool.

SCOTT John, married, 28 years, forester, born Fowlis, Perth. Living at 10 Canford Street, Great Canford, Poole area, Dorset. 1851 census. With Elizabeth, wife, 27 yrs. Mary MALCOLM, niece, 8 years, both born Kingston on Thames, Surrey. Reel HO 107.

SCOTT William, unmarried, 30 years, journeyman upholsterer, born Greenock. Lodger in Mrs. Grace TAYLOR household, 22 Stoneygate, Preston. 1851 census.

SEATON Jane Martin, wife of John late of Dumfries, died at Mittford 30th June 1887 age 63 years, and John her husband, died in Birmingham 24th May 1891 age 69 years. Burial at St. Barnabas and St. Nicholas, Burmington, Warks.

SHAIN James E. husband of Ann BURNS, see BURNS Ann for details.

SHARP Daniel, son of Robert Sharp, merchant of Rothesay, died 12th May, 1820 (36). From "Liverpool Epitaphs" MSS J. Gibson, vol. 5 Scotch Church, Oldham Street, (presb.) Ref. L'pl record office H929 GIB.

SHEPHERD William, of Aberdeen, died 3rd June 1855, age 47 years. St. James, Liverpool.

SHOLTON or SHOTTON Margaret, wife of Andrew POLLOCK, see POLLOCK John for details.

SIMM Robert born 7th November 1800, baptised, 21st November 1802, 3rd son of James Simm, mariner, native of Burnt Island, by his wife Ann HUNTER, native of Gateshead. St. Hilda's, South Shields, Co Durham, baptisms.

SINCLAIR Joseph, born 27th August 1808, baptised 4th September 1808, 3rd son of David Sinclair, farmer, native of Preston, Lancs., and Jane, his wife, late MORGAN, native of Edinburgh. Bishopwearmouth, Co Durham, baptisms.

SINCLAIR George, unmarried, 50 or 30 years, brushmaker, born Edinburgh. Lodging with William THOMPSON, 5 Stoneygate, Preston. 1851 census.

SINCLAIR William only son of Robert and Mary Sinclair, formerly of Gourock, Scotland, died Liverpool 25th May 1861 age 16 years. St. James, Liverpool.

SLATER Christopher, head, married, 64 years, mariner, born Shetland. 167 Adelaide Street, 1881 census Westoe and Jarrow, Co Durham. St. Marks.

SMEATH George, 34, yrs. gold beater, born Edinburgh. Phebe, wife 33 yrs. born Birmingham. 17 Bridge St. Manchester. 1851 census.

SMILEE Margaret, 28 years, born Calder, Scotland. 1851 census,
Northallerton, Yorks. Gaol - Staff. Reel HO 107/2377 folio 400.

SMITH George, unmarried, 23 years, born Rosehearty, Scotland.
Police Station, Rusholme. 1871 census, Rusholme.

SMITH Isabella, born 4th April 1801, baptised 17th July 1803,
6th dau. of James Smith, labourer, native of Dundee, by his
wife, WIGHTON, native of the same place. St. Hilda's, South
Shields, Co Durham, baptisms.

SMITH James of Bressey, Shetland. Died 27th March 1858 age 36
years. St. James, Liverpool.

SMITH James T. married, 43 years, commissioned boat man, coast
guard, born Slens Castle, Aberdeenshire in 1861 census (in 1871
census, place of birth given as Cruden, Aberdeenshire). Living
at Bay, St. Margarets at Cliffe, Kent. With Jane, wife, 40
years, born Plymouth, Devon. Children, James F., 12 years. Mary
Ann, 11 years, both born Margate, Kent. Jane, 7 years. Matilda,
4 years, both born Deal, Kent. William, 10 months, born St.
Margarets. 1861 census. Reel RG9/547.

SMITHERN Alfred Henry, born 21st January 1879, baptised 1st June
1879, son of Charles Smithern, goldsmith, and Elizabeth PROCTOR,
of 4 Lestre? Place, Stockbridge, Edinburgh. St. Lukes, Newcastle
upon Tyne, baptisms.

SPARLING living at south foreland lighthouse, St. Margarets at
Cliffe, Kent. 1881 census. James Sparling, 31 years, engineer in
charge of lighthouse, born Hacklife? Beds. With Emily, 28 years,
born Stirling, Scotland. Children, James C., 4 years, born
Penzance. Emily B. 1 year, born St. Albans, Herts. Reel
RG11/1002.

SPEIRS Helen dau. of late Archibald Speirs Esq. of Elderslie,
Renfrewshire, born 4th October 1801, died Leamington 10th April
1887. M.I. from St. James, Milverton, Warks.

SPEIRS Mary dau. of Archibald Speirs of Elderslie, Renfrewshire,
died Leamington 1839 age 40 years. M.I. from St. James,
Milverton, Warks.

SPENCER Margaret, 68 years, widow, servant, glass polisher, born
Glasgow. 166 Spring Gardens, Public House. 1851 census, Bolton.
Reel 2211 In folio 493a.

STEPHEN James, son of James native of Boddam, Aberdeenshire, and
late Master of "Duncan Ritchie" of Glasgow, died in Liverpool
11th December 1848 age 27 years. "Liverpool Epitaphs" MSS J.
Gibson, vol. 3 St. Michaels, Pitt Street, C of E.

STEVENSON Agnes Margaret of Glasgow, born 29th September 1915,
died 19th May 1971. M.I. from Knowle Parish Church, Warks.

STEWART Elizabeth (Mrs. Hird) born 1904, Glasgow, died October
1986, Province, dau of John and Elizabeth A. (McQUADE)
Stewart. U.S.A. Obituaries, Sun Chronicle, Rhode Island.

STEWART Jane, wife of George INNES, see INNES John for details.

STEWART Jane, wife of James THORNLEY, see THORNLEY James for
details.

STEWART Jane Falconer, wife of James Gordon Stewart, died 11th
March 1859 in her 32nd year. The two preceding were great
grandson and granddau. of Jean THOM, see THOM. William 2nd son
of James Gordon Stewart and Jane Falconer Stewart, died 22nd
June 1858, 1 year 10 months. St. James, Liverpool, Necropolis,
nonconformists.

STOBY living at 2 St. Annes Place, Manchester, 1851 census.
William Stoby, 71 years, widower. Jane, 42 years, niece,
unmarried. Margaret, 22 years, niece, unmarried. William,
nephew, 20 years, unmarried, all born Crieff, Scotland.

STONES living at Burnden, Bolton. 1851 census. Samuel Stones, 37
years, starch maker at bleach works, born Farnworth. Mary Ann,
42 years, born Glasgow. Children, Jane, 18 years, stitcher in
bleach works, born Bolton. Christiana, 16 years, dress maker,
born Great Lever, Bolton. Reel 2211 Ib folio 543a.

STORRER Michael, 29 years, of Kinghorn, Fifeshire, rectifier,
died in Smith Street, Parish of St. John, of apoplexy. No. 13
26th January 1830, ward D, No. 76. Westgate General Cemetery,
Elswick, Newcastle upon Tyne. Interments.

SUTHERLAND Adam, widow, 55 years, retired surgeon, born
Montrose, Scotland. 41 Longfleet, Poole area, Dorset, 1851
census. With Philip, son unmarried, 19 years, medical student,
born Hayes, Middlesex. Mary M. dau., unmarried, 17 years, at
home, born Hayes, Middlesex. George R., son, 13 years, born St.
Giles, London.

SUTHERLAND living at 39 Wigan Road, Atherton? Lancs. 1871
census. Samuel Sutherland, 41 years, machine maker. Christian,
wife 40 years. Samuel, son, 18 years, apprentice. Joan, dau., 15
years. Jane, dau., 12 years. Decima M., 8 years, all born
Aberdeen. James, 3 years, son, born Atherton.

SUTOR John, unmarried, 32 years, born Sanquhar, Scotland.
Lodging with Elizabeth TUCKER, publican. 1861 census, Village,
St. Margarets at Cliffe, Kent. Reel RG HO 107/1632.

TATE John, Lenskill Street, native of Lerwick, master sailor, 85
years. Buried 20th October 1836. Tynemouth, Christ Church,
Northumberland. Burials.

TEMPLEMAN John, born 13th January 1793, baptised, 13th August,
1807, 6th son of John Templeman, soldier, native of Cork, and
Mary, his wife, late MACLOUD, native of Perth, Scotland.
Bishopwearmouth, Co Durham, baptisms.

THOBURN James of Newgate Street, parish of St. Andrew, linen draper and son of Robert and Agnes Thoburn of Douglas, Lanarkshire, died of Typhoid fever. No. 217, 13th October 1831, ward P, No. 142, 26 years. Westgate Cemetery, Elswick, Newcastle upon Tyne. Interments.

THOM David, D.D. born at Glasgow 19th February 1795, died Liverpool, 27th February 1862. For 40 years minister of the Gospel. John his only son, killed by a fall while descending Scuir-na-Gillian, Isle of Skye, 2nd September 1870 age 30 years. St. James, Liverpool, the Necropolis, nonconformists.

THOM Robert, was brother of Rev. David Thom D.D. see above. He published "chinese vocabulary", "chinese speaker". Translations into chinese of Aesops Fables and "translation of a chinese tail" which has appeared in Germany.

THOM John David, son of David and Euphemia Thom, died 3rd November 1836 age 17 months. Margaret Steele Thom, 1st wife of Rev. David Thom, died 22nd October 1832 age 34. Margaret Steele Thom 2nd dau. of above, died 17th January 1834 age 20 months. Mary Jane 4th dau. of Rev. David and Euphemia Thom. Died 22nd June 1846 age 23 months. St. James, Liverpool, the Necropolis, nonconformists.

THOM Jean (FALCONER) widow of John Thom, merchant, Glasgow and mother of Robert Thom Esq. H.B.M. Consul at Ningpo, China. She was born at Glasgow 22nd January 1768, died Liverpool 6th December 1847 age 79. St. James, Liverpool, the Necropolis, nonconformists.

THOM Margaret, wife of George Charles CORSE, and last surviving child of John and Jean Thom, died 21st November 1872 age 70 years. George Charles, died 4th April 1877 age 74 years. St. James, Liverpool, the Necropolis, nonconformists.

THOMPSON Janet, wife of John MUIR, see Muir Janet for details.

THOMPSON George, born 30th November 1802, baptised 23rd January 1803, 2nd son of Thomas THOMPSON, mariner, native of Grange Pans, North Britain, by his wife Jane BLACKBIRD, native of Reyton. St. Hilda's South Shields, Co Durham. Baptisms.

THOMPSON living at 56 Byron Street, Carlisle. 1851 census. Margaret Thompson, widow, 50 years, born Annan, Scotland. Children, Francis, unmarried, 22 years, flesher, butchers. Mary, unmarried, 36 years, bobbin/mach. Jessie, married 20 years, cotton fact. Margaret, married, 18 years, cotton fact. George, unmarried, 16 years, piecer. Joseph, 11 years. Robert, 9 years. All born Scotland. John SKELTON, son, 7 years, born Stockport. Jane McGARVIN, dau., 3 months, born Carlisle.

THOMPSON Robert, married, 35 years, stone mason, born Lesbarnet? Scotland. 1851 census Chorley, Lancs. Town Reel 2263 folio 120.

THOMPSON James, born 27th April 1812, baptised 31st May 1812, 4th son of Thos. Thompson, cordwainer, native of Dunbar, North Britain, by his wife, Margaret, dau. of Alex. PURVES, native of Earlston, North Britain. St. John's, Newcastle upon Tyne, baptisms.

THOMPSON Alexander, born 10th December ???? baptised 31st May 1812, 3rd son of Thos. Thompson, see above.

THOMPSON Thomas, born 18th January ???? baptised 31st May 1812, 2nd son of Thos. Thompson, see above.

THOMSON William, brother in law of I.K. CAMPBELL, see CAMPBELL I.K. for details.

THORNLEY living at Blair Row, Kiersley. 1851 census. James Thornley, 36 years, labourer in chemical works, born Manchester. Jane, wife, (formerly STEWART), 35 years, born Glasgow. Children, Susannah, 17 years, slubber. Isabel, 15 years, slubber. James, 13 years, all born Manchester. John, 11 years. Harriot, 8 years. Margaret, 6 years. Sandy, 3 years. William, 1 year, all born Kiersley. Jane STEWART, mother, born Glasgow.

TOGGART?, 60 years, shipwright, born Kelso, Scotland. Living at 4 Thompson Street, Whitehaven. Holy Trinity 1851 census. With Rachel, wife, 59 years, born Whitehaven.

TURNBULL George of Glasgow. Margaret Alison his wife died November 12th 1856, age 22 years. St. James, Liverpool.

TURNBULL William, born 5th February 1808, baptised 1st January 1809, 2nd son of James Turnbull, glassmaker, native of Dunbarton, and Ann his wife, late WILKINSON, native of Monkwearmouth. Bishopwearmouth, Co Durham, baptisms.

TURNS Elizabeth, wife of George ANDERSON, see ANDERSON George for details.

UNION Jane, wife of James BLACK, see BLACK Margaret for details.

VALS? Cath, mother in law of Robert CURRIE, see CURRIE for details.

WALLACE Robert, born 19th June 1802, baptised 14th November 1802, 1st son of Robert WALLACE, mariner, native of Methell, Fifeshire, North Britain, by his wife Dorothy HALES, native of this place. St. Hilda's, South Shields, Co Durham, baptisms.

WALLACE Elizabeth, born 9th January 1804, baptised 12th August 1804, 1st dau. of Robert Wallace, see above.

WALLACE James of Stranraer, Wigtownshire, died 2nd November 1855 age 38 years. St. James, Liverpool.

WANNAN Janet, widow of William MARTIN, native of Dundee, died at Broughty Ferry, Forfar, on 28th Dec. 1850 (68) interred here. "Liverpool Epitaphs" MSS J. Gibson, vol. 5, Scotch Church, (cont)

Rodney Street, (presb.) Ref. L'pl record office H929 GIB.

WATSON George, born 19th October 1803, baptised 21st November 1803, 1st dau.(?) of Patrick Watson, surgeon, native of Dundee, Scotland, by his wife Jane TARSE? native of Newcastle upon Tyne. St. Hilda's, South Shields, Co Durham, baptisms.

WATSON Elizabeth dau. of John and Janet Watson of Dinlabyre, Roxburghshire, died 4th December 1829 age 22 years. Isabella MacDonald KAYE lost on passage there to Prince Edward Island in spring 1846 age 49 years. George Watson, merchant of Liverpool, died 15th February 1853 age 47 years. Christian Oliver, wife of above George Watson, died 17th June 1854 age 44 years. Andrew Watson, son of above John and Janet Watson, died 15th June - age 57 years. James MACDONALD only son of Isabella MacDonald in Isle of Madeira 1859 age 33 years. St. James, Liverpool, the Necropolis, nonconformists.

WEBSTER Jane, born 22nd January 1846, Peterhead, Aberdeen. Father Thomas Webster, a wright, mother Jane COOPER. Married Frederick COPPIN at Parish Church, Shirley, Surrey, 23rd December 1875. Both full age and residents of Addington, Surrey. Records of Mr. A.J.F. COPPIN, 71 High View Road, Guildford, Surrey. GU2 5RU.

WEDDERSPOON Andrew, a native of the city of Perth, born 7th August 1812, died 8th June 1842. From "Liverpool Epitaphs" MSS, J. Gibson, vol. 5, Scotch Church, Rodney Street, (presb.) Ref. L'pl record office H929 GIB.

WELSH Thomas died 23rd April 1829 (79). Son of late John Welsh, Morton Mains, Dumfriesshire and grand uncle to John Welsh, all interred here. From "Liverpool Epitaphs" MSS, J. Gibson, vol. 5, Scotch Church, Oldham Street, (presb.) Ref. L'pl record office H929 GIB.

WHITE living at 36 York Street, St. Margarets, Westminster, 1861 census. Peter White, married, 40 years, bootmaker, born Kilmarnock, Scotland. Mary, wife, 34 years, shoe binder, born Glasgow. Children, John, 16 years, labourer, deaf, born Edinburgh. Elizabeth, 14 years, shoe binder. Sophy, 12 years. Peter, 9 years. Eliza, 7 years. Mary Ann, 3 years. Alexander, 4 months, all born London. From Essex FHS.

WHITE Christina Douglas Fairless, wife of William DEAN, see DEAN Christina Douglas Fairless for details.

WHITEHOUSE In memory of Marie Anna WEISSE, dau. of Traucott Heinrich Weisse and Sophie MARQHIDORFF his wife born in Edinburgh, October 20th 1852, died Guildford, January 10th 1945. For many years schoolmistress at Eton and then at Northlands in this parish. In Memory of Henry Victor WHITEHOUSE formerly WEISSE, born Edinburgh May 1sr 1859, died London October 7th 1935. Peggie the dau. of Henry and Margaret Weisse born May 21st 1899 died January 2nd 1913. M.I. Christchurch, Virginia Water, Surrey.

WHITELOW Peter, 25 years, plasterer, born Glasgow. Living at 75 Howell Croft, Bolton. 1851 census. With Elizabeth, wife, 24 years, born Glasgow. Children, John, 3 years. Alexander, 5 months, both born Bolton. Reel 14 2211 IL folio 405.

WIGHTMAN living at Foundry Street, Warrington, 1851 census. Robert Wightman, 28 years, stonemason, born Dumfries. Janet, wife, 25 years, born Kirkcudbright. Margaret, dau., 4 months, born Wigan.

WIGHTON, wife of James SMITH, see SMITH Isabella for details.

WILLIAMSON Margaret, born 8th March 1801, baptised 19th August 1804, 2nd dau. of John Williamson, mariner, native of Cooper, North Britain, by his wife Margaret WATSON, native of this place. St. Hilda's, South Shields, Co Durham, baptisms.

WILLIAMSON Ann, born 9th May 1803, baptised 19th August 1804, 3rd dau. of above.

WILSON living at Rawhead, Barton, Nr. Penrith, Cumb. 1851 census. Felix Wilson, married 56 years, chain maker, born Dumfries. Janet, wife, 45 years, born Shaw, Renfrewshire.

WILSON Isabella, born 28th March 1809, baptised, 23rd April 1809, 1st dau. of John Wilson, blacksmith, native of Edinburgh, and Isabella his wife, late HUNTER, native of Swalwell. Bishopwearmouth, Co Durham, baptisms.

WILSON Robert, born 4th May 1807, baptised 10th January 1808, 1st son of John Wilson, as above.

WILSON Captain John, of Tyninghame, Scotland, died December, 1830, age 44 years. St. James, Liverpool, the Necropolis, nonconformists.

WILSON Kenneth, born Glasgow 1859, died 10th December 1894. M.I. from Smethwick Old Church, Staffs.

WILSON Ann, wife of Richard PUNSHOW, see PUNSHOW Sarah for details.

WILSON Thomas, unmarried, 45 years, f. labourer, born Glasgow. Stokesley Union Workhouse, North Riding of Yorkshire. 1881 census.

WINCHESTER Ann, wife of Robert Winchester of Grantown, North Britain, died Liverpool 28th June 1878 age 71 years. St. James, Liverpool, the Necropolis, nonconformists.

WITT Jane, unmarried, 16 years, house servant to Rbt. FIDLER of Stokesley, born Dundee. 1851 census, Stokesley, North Riding of Yorkshire. Reel HO107/2376.

WOOD Andrew son of John and Isabella Wood, native of Dunbar, late of ship "Torry? Dixon" of the port, died at Milburn Place, 18 yrs. Buried 22nd Feb. 1837. Tynemouth, Christ Church, Northd.

WOOD living at Northallerton, Yorks. 1851 census. George Wood, 23 years, born Northallerton, Yorks. Isabella, wife, 21 years, born Moffat, Scotland. Reel HO107/2377 folio 379.

WOODS Richard, born at Fullarton, Ayrshire on September 12th 1821, died at Clipstone Park (NTT) on June 7th 1886. Edwinstowe, Churchyard Memorials (NTT).

WRIGHT living at Sankey Green, Warrington, 1851 census. John Wright, 50 years, wheelwright, born Dumfries. Margaret, wife, 49 years, born Dumfries. Children, David, 18 years, born Eccles. Margaret, 16 years. Frances, 14 years. Robert, 10 years, all born Warrington.

WRIGHT living at Stokesley, North Riding of Yorkshire, 1881 census. Thomas Wright, married, 45 years, carpenter, born Nunthorpe, Yorkshire. Agnes, wife, 42 years, born Dumfriesshire. Children, Kate, 13 years. Annie, 9 years. Thomas William, 6 years. Sarah Ellen, 4 years, all born Stokesley.

WYLIE Rev. David Stewart, more than 60 years a preacher of the Gospel, died 6th August 1856 age 86 years. Jean JAMIESON his wife, died 25th September 1851 age 83 years. Manuscript note - Originally Minister of a Secession Church at Burntshields, Nr. Kilbarchan, Renfrewshire, 1793-6, afterwards of a Congregation of Independants at Paisley 1796-9, then to Liverpool for 40 years. St. James, Liverpool, the Necropolis, nonconformists.

WYLLIE Hugh Y. born 1898, Kilmarnach. Died September 1986, Wheaton, Illinois, son of James and Jeannie (YOUNG) Wyllie. U.S.A. obituaries, Sun Chronicle, Rhode Island.

YORKE living at Bishop Middleham, Co Durham. 1851 census. Thomas H. Yorke, vicar, 66 years, born Halton Place, Yorkshire. Maria, wife, 63 years, born Edinburgh. Maria A.S. OGILVY, sister in law, 68 years, born Edinburgh. Elizabeth CONNEL, servant, unmarried, 38 years, born Perth. Reel HO107/2384 folio 723.

YOUNG Adam, born Selkirk, North Britain. 26th August 1803, died St Leonards 4th September 1876. Anne MEABURN, wife, born 6th December 1818, died 4th March 1899. M.I. Boston, Lincs. cemetery

YOUNG Alexander Esq. of Aberdeen, died 5th Oct. 1821 (in 44th year). From "Liverpool Epitaphs" MSS, J. Gibson, vol. 5, Scotch Church, Oldham Street (presb.) Ref. L'pl record office, H929 GIB

YOUNG Jeannie, wife of James WYLLIE, see WYLLIE Hugh Y. for details.

YOUNG Matthew, Smith St. parish of St. John, rectifier, son of Andrew and Isabella Young of Halbeath, Fifeshire, died of Suppresion of Urine age 51. No. 218, 16th Dec. 1831, ward D, No 75. Westgate Cem. Elswick, Newcastle-u-Tyne, interments.

ADDAMS James, married, 32 years, ships mate, born Scotland. Sailors Home, 44 Stuart Street, Docks, Cardiff. 1881 census.

AGNEW living at 90 Simpsons Court, Carlisle. 1851 census. John Agnew, 29 years, blacksmith, born Rocliffe, Cumberland. Jannet, wife, 24 years, born Scotland. George, son, 2 years, born Scotland.

AITKEN Isabella Johnson, spinster, Linteford, district of Tanfield in the Co of Durham, a native of Scotland, died of consumption. No. 3837, buried 25th April 1888, ward B, No. 101, depth 6 feet, age 23 years. Westgate cemetery, Newcastle-u-Tyne.

ALLAN William, born 10th September 1804, baptised 30th December 1804, 2nd son of William ALLAN (ALLEIN?), mariner, native of North Britain, by his wife Margaret BULMER, native of Bratton, Yorkshire. St. Hilda's, South Shields, Co Durham, baptisms.

ALLEN John, 22 years, lodger, unmarried, tailor, born Scotland. 14 Ridgeway gates, Bolton. 1851 census, reel 2211 IK folio 368.

ALLEN John, born 2nd September 1802, baptised 6th March 1803, 1st son of William ALLEN, mariner, native of North Britain, by his wife, Margaret BULMER, native of Brothen Yorks. St. Hilda's, South Shields, Co Durham, baptisms. See ALLAN William.

ALLEN James, 47 years, weaver, born Scotland, visitor in household of William WREN, see WREN William. 219 Pattinsons Lane, Carlisle, 1851 census.

ALSTON Anne, 15 years, born Scotland. Niece of Andrew ROSS, 24 years, unmarried, iron mongers assistant, born Hull, Yorkshire. 43 Melbourne Street, Newcastle upon Tyne, East All Saints, 1871 census.

ANDERSON Alexander, 14 years, scholar, born Scotland. Inmate of Garth Heads Ragged and Industrial School. 1871 census, Newcastle upon Tyne, East All Saints.

ANDERSON living at Chapel Buildings, Newcastle upon Tyne, 1871 census, East All Saints. Jane Anderson, head, widow, 43 years, born Northumberland. Children, David, 20 years, engineer, born Bedlington, Northumberland. Henrietta, 15 years, pottery girl. Robert, 12 years, both born Scotland. Margaret, 9 years. William, 5 years, both born Newcastle. John BATEY, son in law, 26 years, stoker, born Newcastle. Isabella BATEY, dau., 22 years, born Bedlington. Jane Isabella Batey, grand dau., 2 months, born Newcastle.

ANDERSON living at 7 New Road, Newcastle upon Tyne. 1871 census, East All Saints. James Anderson, married, 28 years, medical student, born Chelmsford, Essex. Mary, wife, 30 years, born Newcastle. James, son, 1 year, born Newcastle. John, father, 60 years, annuitant, born Scotland. Elizabeth, mother, 60 years, born London. Sarah, sister, unmarried, 19 years, housekeeper, born Berwick on Tweed.

ANDREWS William, 30 years, carver and gilder, born Scotland.
Lodging at Queen Street, Bolton. 1841 census.

ARMSTRONG living at Parkham Beck, Carlisle. 1851 census. John
Armstrong, head, 36 years, weaver, born Scotland. Sarah, wife,
38 years, born Scotland. Children, Isabella, 15 years, weaver,
born Scotland. Daniel, 3 years, born Carlisle. John, 11 years,
born Scotland. Andrew, 6 months, born Carlisle. John CUNNINGHAM,
visitor, married, 26 years, born Scotland. John McREY, visitor,
unmarried, 48 years, born Scotland.

ARMSTRONG Sarah, unmarried, 16 years, groom, born Scotland.
Servant in house of David NIXON, 214 Willow Holme, Carlisle.
1851 census.

ASTBURY Mary A. 14 years, house servant, born Scotland.
Westfield Street, Township of Eccleston, (St. Helens), Lancs.
1851 census.

ATKIN Mary, dau. of George MOLLONS, see MOLLONS for details.

ATKINSON Margaret, 13 years, born Scotland. Niece of Thomas
Atkinson, born Warwick. Inn keeper. 27 Bridges Caldew, Carlisle.
1851 census.

AUSTIN living at Stokesley, North Riding of Yorkshire. 1881
census. John Austin, widower, 54 years, labourer, born Hythe,
Kent. Amelia, dau., widow, 25 years, born Vauxhall, London.
Edward, son, 17 years, labourer, born Scotland.

BAKER James, born 7th April 1803, baptised 23rd September, 1804,
1st son of William Baker, mariner, native of North Britain, by
his wife Mary CUNNINGHAM native of this place. St. Hilda's,
South Shields, Co Durham, baptisms.

BAMBER living at 71 Denton Holme, Carlisle. 1851 census. Henry
Bamber, married, 24 years, born Manchester. Jane, wife, 19
years, born Scotland. James, son, 1 year, born Scotland.

BARR living at 7 Denton Hill, Carlisle. 1851 census. James Barr,
married, 43 years, dyer. Jennet, wife, 43 years. Children, John,
14 years, dyer. Mary, 12 years. James, 10 years, all born
Scotland.

BAXTER Janet, unmarried, 26 years, matron of industrial school,
born Scotland. Garth Heads Ragged and Industrial School,
Newcastle upon Tyne. 1871 census, East All Saints.

BAYNES Thomas, born 20th May 1789, baptised 9th October 1804,
2nd son of Thomas Baynes, tailor, native of North Britain, by
his wife Eleanor STOKELL, native of this place. St. Hilda's,
South Shields, Co Durham, baptisms.

BEATON living at Nob Row, Bolton. 1851 census. Neal Beaton, 32 years, operative chemist. Margaret, wife, 32 years, paper works. Children, Jane, 12 years. Sarah, 10 years. Thomenea, 8 years. Janett, 6 years. Mary, 4 years, all born Scotland. Hannah, 1 year, born Bolton, Little Lever. Reel 2211 2Cd folio 583a-584.

BEAUMONT Mathew, married, 33 years, weaver, born Scotland. Living at 23 Bridge Lane, Carlisle, 1851 census. With Sarah, wife, 32 years. Ann Lightfoot, dau., 4 years, both born Carlisle

BELL Charles, married, 38 years, cartman, born Scotland. Living at 7 Blagdon Street, Newcastle upon Tyne, 1871 census, East All Saints. With Elizabeth, wife, 34 years, tailoress. Children, George, 13 years. Jessie, 11 years. Charles, 9 years. Stewart, 7 years. William, 5 years. Matthew, 3 years. Robert, 7 months. All born Newcastle.

BELL William, married, 64 years, weaver, born Scotland. Living at Caldcoats, Carlisle. 1851 census. With Ellenor, wife, 60 years, winder. Sarah, dau., unmarried, 18 years, factory. Mary BLAKE, grand dau., 6 years. All born Carlisle.

BELL Rebecca, unmarried, 17 years, house servant, born Scotland. In house of Thomas ISMAY, innkeeper. 98 Bridge Lane, Carlisle. 1851 census.

BELL William, Grand son in law of William SEATON, see SEATON for details.

BERRIE John, 31 years, dyer, employer, born Scotland. Living at 12 Olham Street, Manchester. 1851 census, St. Pauls. With Caroline, 20 years, wife, born Holt, Norfolk. Caroline D. dau., 1 month, born Manchester. Reel 2229.

BINGLEY living at 24 Bengal Street, Keighley, Yorkshire. 1881 census. Elizabeth Bingley, wife of George (wool factory), and James, son, 9 years, both born Scotland.

BIRRELL Andrew, head, widower, 78 years, labourer, born Scotland living at 31 Caldew Side, Carlisle. 1851 census. With Catherine GRAHAM, dau., widow, 30 years, housekeeper. Mary GRAHAM, granddau., 11 years. George GRAHAM, grandson, 8 years, all born Carlisle.

BLACKLOCK Annie, unmarried, 29 years, cert. schoolmistress, born Scotland. 1881 census, Stokesley, North Riding of Yorkshire.

BLAKE James, unmarried, 39 years, shoe maker, born Scotland. Lodger in house of Richard DAVIDSON. 42 Byron Street, Carlisle. 1851 census.

BOND William, married, 62 yrs, weaver, born Scotland. Living at Parkham Beck, Caldergate, Trinity, Carlisle, 1851 census. With Eliz., wife, 56 yrs, winder, born Northb. Eliz. ROBINSON, dau., married, 27 yrs, weaver, born Scotland. William ROBINSON, son in law, 36 yrs, fireman, born Cumb. Grandchildren, Wm. 10 yrs. Eliz. 3 yrs. John, 1 year, all born Carlisle. Page 37.

BOND John, married, 31 years, weaver, born Scotland. Living at
204 Parkham Beck, Carlisle. 1851 census. With Mary, wife, 26
years, bobbin winder, born Alston C., William, son, 9 years, and
Elizabeth, dau., 6 years, both born Carlisle.

BONNER William, married 75 years, tailor, born Scotland. Living
at 91 Bridge Lane, Carlisle. 1851 census. With Mary, wife, 83
years, born Hesket, Cmb. Rachel KIRKPATRICK, grand dau., house
servant, born Carlisle.

BOWIE living at 70 Denton Holme, Carlisle. 1851 census. John
Bowie, married, 32 years, dyer. Rebecca, wife, 33 years. John,
son, 5 years. All born Scotland. Rebecca, dau., 2 years, born
Carlisle. Margaret McFARLANE, wifes sister, 14 years, factory,
born Carlisle.

BOXLAND living at 202 Parkam Beck, Carlisle. 1851 census. John
Boxland, married, 27 years, shoemaker, born Scotland. Jemima,
wife, 23 years, born Liverpool. Mary, dau., 2 years, born
Scotland.

BOYES living at 11 Henry Street, Bedford, Lancs. 1871 census.
John Boyes, 31 years, joiner. Eliz. wife, 30 years. Children
James, 7 years. David, 5 years. John, 3 years. Peter, 1 year.
All born Scotland.

BRADLEY Edward, 11 or 14 years, scholar, born Scotland. Inmate
of Garth Heads Ragged and Industrial Schools. 1871 census,
Newcastle upon Tyne, East All Saints.

BRADLEY living at 48 Caldcoats, Carlisle. 1851 census. Peter
Bradley, married, 83 years, weaver, born Ireland. Ellen, Wife,
weaver, born Scotland. John, son, unmarried, 42 years, born
Scotland. Ellen, niece, 14 years, born Cumb.

BRODIE Peter, married, 40 years, seaman, born Scotland. Living
at 56 Gibson Street, Newcastle upon Tyne, 1871 census, East All
Saints. With Margaret, wife, 32 years, born Scotland. Children,
William, 13 years. Peter, 5 years. James, 2 years, all born
Newcastle.

BROWN George, unmarried, 19 years, potter, born Scotland.
Lodging at Westfield Street, Eccleston, St. Helens, Lancs. 1851
census.

BROWN living at Parkham Beck, Carlisle. 1851 census. John Brown,
married, 46 years, coppersmith. Mary, wife, 45 years. Catherine,
dau., 25 years, bobbin winder. All born Scotland. Margaret,
dau., 7 years, born Carlisle.

BROWN John, unmarried, 22 years, baker, born Scotland. Visitor
in house of Jos. HARRISON, 124 Watson Court, Carlisle. 1851
census.

BROWN Helen born 9th March 1803, bapt. 26th Jan. 1804, 2nd dau.
of Robert Brown, wherryman, native of North Britain, by his wife
Elizabeth HIND, native of this place. St. Hilda's, South Shields

BROWN James, unmarried, 42 years, mate in M.S. born Scotland.
Living at Sailors Home, 44 Stuart Street, Docks, Cardiff, 1881
census.

BROWN Janet, wife of Richard SHILLINGLAW, see SHILLINGLAW for
details.

BROWN Jonathan, unmarried, 28 years, mariner, born Scotland.
Lodging in house of Joseph RANDELL. 212 Quay, Poole area,
Dorset. 1851 census.

BUCHANAN David, late of Scotland who departed this life on the
2nd day of August 1862 aged 63 years, and was interred here 6th
August 1862. Also John Buchanan of Spring Terrace, Ramsbottom
who departed this life on 5th day of December 1865 age 70 years.
Next to above grave is a HUTTON grave with Ann the wife of John
Buchanan of Spring Terrace died 7th May 1860. St. Andrews Parish
Church, Ramsbottom.

BUCHANNAN John, married, 57 years, warper. Living at 173 Church
Street, Carlisle. 1851 census. With Elizabeth, wife, 54 years,
both born Scotland. Isabella, dau. unmarried, 21 years, born
Carlisle.

BURGESS George, married, 39 years, weaver, born Scotland. Living
at Caldcoats, Carlisle. 1851 census. With Ann, wife, 32 years,
weaver. Children, Mary, 19 years. Richard, 14 years, Henry, 10
years, Jannet, 7 years. John, 4 years, Andrew, 2 years, all born
Carlisle.

BURGESS John, married, 43 years, weaver, born Scotland. Living
at Caldcoats, Carlisle, 1851 census. With Margaret, wife, 40
years, born Cumbria. Children, Andrew, 19 years. Mary, 14 years.
Fergus, 10 years. Elizabeth, 7 years. Margaret, 4 years. Jane, 9
months, all born Carlisle.

BURGESS Richard Ross, married, 34 years, bank manager, born
Scotland. Living at Stokesley, North Riding of Yorkshire. 1851
census. With Sarah, wife, 31 years, born Scotland. Children,
Allan Grant, 4 years. Fanny Kay, 2 years. Mary, 1 year. All born
Stokesley.

BURRELL Henry Thomas, 23 years, printers compositor, born
Scotland. Living in the house of Jane DEVLIN. 32 Victoria Place,
Newcastle upon Tyne. 1871 census, East All Saints.

CAIRD living at 7 Dale Street, Manchester. 1851 census. John
Caird, 45 years, draper. Margaret, wife, 43 years, both born
Scotland.

CAMERON Hugh, 38 years, pipemaker, born Scotland. Living at 14
Newtown, Whitehaven. 1851 census, Holy Trinity. With, Eliz. 34
years, wife, born Distington, Cumb. Children, James, 12 years.
William, 10 years. Eliz. 7 years. Sarah, 5 years. John, 2 years.
Daniel, 5 weeks. All born Whitehaven.

CAMPBELL living at 12 Suffolk St, Birmingham. 1851 census St.
Philip. Thomas Campbell, 21 years, traveller, visitor in house.
Jonn Campbell, married, 25 years, professor of dancing. Lodger.
Ann Campbell, 26 years, domestic, all born Scotland. House of
Martha RAMSDEN. En 9, sch 74, page 276.

CAMPBELL Christopher, unmarried, 20 years, brassfinisher, born
Scotland. Lodging at 17 Buxton Street, Newcastle upon Tyne. 1871
census, East All Saints. House of Henry HENNESSY.

CAMPBELL James, married, 63 years, labourer, born Scotland. 1851
census Carlisle. With Ellenor, wife, 52 years, and James, son,
22 years, joiner. Jane dau., 20 years, all born Cumbria.

CAMPBELL living at 54 Gibson Street, Newcastle upon Tyne. 1871
census, East All Saints. Maria Campbell, head, married, 57
years, seamans wife. Thomas, son, 11 years, both born Scotland.
Catherine, grand-daughter, 9 months, born Newcastle.

CARMICHAEL living at 3 Grenville Terrace, Newcastle upon Tyne.
1871 census, East All Saints. Robert Carmichael, 35 years,
cooper. Mary, wife, 33 years. Robert, son, 4 years. James, son,
2 years. All born Scotland.

CARTER John, widower, 61 years, works at Gas Yard, born
Scotland. Living at 13 Blagden Street, Newcastle upon Tyne. 1871
census, East All Saints. With Mary MOORHEAD, dau., married, 36
years, domestic servant, born Ancroft, Northumberland. Jane
Carter, dau., unmarried, 24 years, dressmaker. Matthew Carter,
nephew, 11 years, errand boy, both born Newcastle.

CHRISHOLM Angus, unmarried, 20 years, engine fitter, born
Scotland. Lodger, Chorley, Lancs. 1851 census, town, reel 2263,
folio 074.

CHISHOLME living at 97 Simpsons Court, Carlisle. 1851 census.
Catherine Chisholme, widow, 52 years, housekeeper. Jane, dau.,
unmarried, 26 years, factory. James, son, unmarried, 20 years,
sawyer, all born Scotland.

CLARK Alexander, married, 22 years, engine fitter, born
Scotland. Living at 47 Melbourne Street, Newcastle upon Tyne.
1871 census, East All Saints. With Elizabeth Ann, wife, 20
years. William Alex., son, 2 years. Janet, dau., 4 months. All
born England.

CLOAG or GLOAG? John, unmarried, 48 years, weaver, born
Scotland. Lodging at house of Andrew NELSON, 139 Jane Street,
Carlisle. 1851 census.

COLLINS living at 43 Industrial Dwellings, Newcastle upon Tyne.
1871 census, East All Saints. Bernard Collins, married, 47 yrs.
pavior. Janet, wife, 44 yrs. Children, Thomas F. unmarried, 23
yrs. machine painter. Joseph, unmarried, 21 yrs. iron moulder.
John, 14 yrs. painters apprentice, all born Scotland. Jas? 11
yrs. David, 8 yrs. Janet, 2 yrs. All born Newcastle.

COOPER Catherine, died Newgate Street, Parish of St. John, a
native of Scotland. Of Cholera, age 50 years. No. 333, 2nd March
1832, ward X, No. 116. Westgate Cem. Elswick, Newcastle upon
Tyne, interments.

CORNEY Peter, married, 28 years, chimney sweep, born Scotland.
Living at Stokesley, North Riding of Yorkshire. 1851 census.
With Jane, wife, 25 years, born Richmond, Yorkshire. John, son,
4 years, born Stockton.

COSH living at Margate, Kent. 1841 census. William Cosh, 40
years, Navy. Margaret, 35 years. James, 10 years. All born
Scotland. Elizabeth, 5 years. William, 3 years. Christianna, 5
months, all born Kent.

COUL William, 30 years, coastguard, born Scotland. Living at
Foster's Alley, Deal, Kent. 1841 census. With Elizabeth, 25
years, William, 11 years. Henry, 9 years. James, 7 years, all
not born in Kent. Margaret, 2 years, Mary, 9 months, both born
in Kent. Reel RG 107/466 folio 10, page 12.

COULAND living at 138 Bread Street, Carlisle. 1851 census.
Larence Couland, married, 45 years, carter. Margaret, wife, 37
years, both born Ireland. Children, Ann, 16 years, factory.
Catherine, 14 years, factory. Mary, 12 years. John, 10 years.
James, 5 years, all born Scotland. Margaret, 3 months, born
Carlisle.

COULTHARD Elizabeth, unmarried, 57 years, washerwoman, born
Scotland. Living at 207 Willow Holme, Caldergate, Carlisle. 1851
census, Trinity, page 57, folio 365.

COUTHARD living at 105 Brewery Row, Carlisle. 1851 census.
George Couthard, married, 60 years, cooper. Mary, wife, 60
years, both born Scotland. Ann, dau., 16 years. Robert,
grandson, 9 years, Jane, grand dau., 7 years, Mary Ann, grand
dau., 1 year, all born Cumbria.

CRANMER William T. grandson of Thomas DYSON. See DYSON for
details.

CRATES? Jane, born 18th April 1803, baptised 18th September
1803, 2nd dau. of John Crates? shoemaker, native of North
Britain, by his wife Frances YOUNG, native of Broadberry. St.
Hilda's, South Shields, Co Durham, baptisms.

CROSBY John, married, 50 years, weaver, born Scotland. Living at
162 Chappel Lane, Carlisle. 1851 census. With Sarah, wife, 62
years, winder, born Whitby, Yorkshire.

CUNNINGHAM John, visitor at house of John ARMSTRONG (see same),
26 years, born Scotland. Parkham Beck, Carlisle. 1851 census.

CUNNINGHAM James, 50 years, draper, born Scotland. Living at
White Cross, Warrington. 1851 census. With Harriet, wife, born
Runcorn. Children, Henry, 15 years, born Warrington. Chs.?
James, 10 years, born Gt. Budworth. Eleanor, 6 years. Thomas W.
both born Warrington. Elizabeth SINCLAIR, niece, 19 years, born
Scotland.

CURRAN living at 9 Blagdon Street, Newcastle upon Tyne. 1871
census, East All Saints. Charles Curran, married, 46 years,
labourer in engine factory. Mary A. wife, 43 years, both born
Scotland. Children, Michael, 18 years. Isabella, 13 years.
Charles, 8 years. Dorothy, 5 years, all born Newcastle.

CUTHBERT Hugh, unmarried, 24 years, baker, born Scotland.
Lodging with John BUCHANNAN (see same) 173 Church Street,
Carlisle. 1851 census.

DAVIDSON Agnes, 7 years, scholar, born Scotland. inmate of Garth
Heads Ragged and Industrial Schools, Newcastle upon Tyne. 1871
census, East All Saints.

DAVIDSON Mathew, married, 32 years, paper ruler, born Scotland.
Son in law of Margaret SCOTT, head, widow, 58 years, born
Newcastle, and living with same at 42 Blagdon Street, Newcastle
upon Tyne. 1871 census, East All Saints. Also at this address,
Margaret SCOTT, unmarried, 22 years, dressmaker, born Newcastle.
Elizabeth DAVIDSON, his wife, 29 years. His children, William,
10 years. John, 8 years. Margaret, 5 years. Anne, 2 years.
Robert, 3 months, all born Newcastle.

DEAN Charles, 50 years, manager of cotton factory, born
Scotland. Living at Old Mill, Little Lever, Bolton. 1851 census.
Reel 14 2211 2Db folio 647a.

DICKIE living at 80 Stock Street, Manchester. 1851 census.
Thomas Dickie, 42 years, master bootmaker. Agnes, 37 years,
wife, both born Scotland. Children, Margaret, 12 years, born
Liverpool. Ebenezer, 9 years, born Manchester. Agnes, 6 years,
born Salford. Thomas, 4 years. Samuel, 2 years, both born
Manchester. Reel 2229.

DICKSON living at Head-oth-Lane, Little Lever Bolton. 1851
census. Agnes Dickson, 57 years, modellers wife, born Scotland.
Ann, dau., 26 years, domestic duties, born Scotland. John, son,
19 years, tarra cotter modeller, born Leeds. Reel 2211 2Cd folio
622.

DIGNAN lodging at 16 Blue Anchor Lane, Carlisle. 1851 census.
House of Edward HUNT (see same). Thomas Dignan, married, 36
years, agri. labourer. Margaret, wife, 35 years, both born
Scotland.

DIXON Ann, born 3rd December 1804, baptised 25th December 1804,
2nd dau. of George Dixon, mariner, native of North Britain, by
his wife Dorothy ROBINSON, native of Hartley. St. Hilda's, South
Shields, Co Durham, baptisms.

DIXON living at Heath Lane, Warrington. 1851 census. William
Dixon, 70 years, joiner. Margaret, wife, 70 years. William, son,
22 years?? John, son, 16 years?? All born Scotland.

DOBBIE John, 43 years, public., born Scotland. Living at 28
Turner Street, Manchester. 1851 census, St. Paul's. With Alice,
wife, 32 years. Ellen Dunn, dau., 10 months. Both born
Manchester. Reel 2229.

DOBIE living at 214 Parkam Beck, Carlisle. 1851 census. James
Dobie, married, 66 years, labourer. Margery, wife, 67 years.
Children, Mary, unmarried, 39 years, cotton fact. Georgina,
unmarried, 25 years, cotton fact. William, grandson, 15 years,
piecer. George, grandson, 9 years. Nelson, grandson, 8 months,
all born Scotland.

DOCK Ann, unmarried, 25 years, weaver, born Scotland. Lodger in
house of Thomas PATTERSON, 45 Byron Street, Carlisle. 1851
census.

DOHERTY living at Eccleston Street, Eccleston, St. Helens,
Lancs. 1851 census. Edward Doherty, 46 years, married, glass
makers, labourer, born Ireland. Bridget, wife, 43 years, born
Ireland. Children, Edward, 22 years, glass maker. Daniel, 7
years. Sarah, 14 years. Grace, 12 years. Mary, 9 years, all born
Scotland.

DOYLE living at 115 Brewery Row, Carlisle. 1851 census. John
Doyle, married, 48 years, iron moulder. Jane, wife, 47 years,
both born Scotland. James, son, married, 27 years, dyer. James
Thoburn, grandson, 5 years. John Graham, grandson, 4 years, all
born Carlisle.

DRUMMOND living at 45 Melbourne Street, Newcastle upon Tyne.
1871 census, East All Saints. Ann Drummond, married, 21 years,
seaman's wife. Margaret, dau., 2 years. Marion, dau., 6 months,
all born Scotland.

DRYNAN? living at Broadstairs, Kent. St. Peter's, Thanet. 1841
census. Coastguard Station. James Drynan? 45 years, coastguard.
Catherine, 35 years. William, 12 years. Charles, 11 years, all
born Scotland. James, 9 years. Mary Ann, 7 years. Alexander, 5
years. Sarah, 2 years, all born Kent. Reel HO 107/468, folio 14
page 20.

DRYSDALE living at Chapel Buildings, Newcastle upon Tyne. 1871
census, East All Saints. Thomas Drysdale, married, 50 years,
horse keeper, born Northumberland, Presson (? Preston, nr. North
Shields). Jane, wife, 46 years. Children, Alexander, 17 years,
cartman. Mary Ann, 15 years, servant. Thomas, 11 years. James, 9
yrs, all born Scotland. William, 7 yrs, born Northd., N.K.

DUCKWORTH William, 17 years, unmarried, greengrocer's ass., born
Scotland. Lodging at Old Hall Street, Bolton. 1851 census. Reel
14 2211 IM folio 459a.

DUDGEON Robert, born 17th September 1800, baptised, 12 June
1803, 2nd son of Robert Dudgeon, taylor, native of North
Britain, by his wife Mary PEET, native of Newbrough,
Northumberland. St. Hilda's, South Shields, Co Durham, baptisms.

DUDGEON William, born 19th May 1803, baptised 12th June 1803,
3rd son of above.

DUFFY Gregory, married, 24 years, weaver, born Scotland. Living
at Caldcoats, Carlisle, 1851 census. With Elizabeth, wife, 23
years, weaver. Children, Mary, 2 years. Alexander, 11 months,
all born Carlisle.

DUNBAR Hugh, married, 27 years, hand loom weaver, born Scotland.
Lodging at 9 John Street, Bolton. 1851 Census. Id folio 144.

DUNCAN Thompson, unmarried, 44 years, Able-seaman, born
Scotland. Living at Sailors Home, 44 Stuart Street, Docks,
Cardiff. 1881 census.

DUNCAN William, unmarried, 47 years, Able-seaman, born Scotland.
Living at Sailors Home, 44 Stuart Street, Docks, Cardiff. 1881
census.

DUNCAN David, born 14th July 1804, baptised 16th September 1805,
3rd son of James Duncan, hairdresser, native of North Britain,
by his wife Jane OLIVER, native of Gateshead. St. Hilda's, South
Shields, Co Durham, baptisms.

DUNCAN living at 6 Grenville Street, Newcastle upon Tyne. 1871
census, East All Saints. John Duncan, married, 56 years? cabinet
maker, born Scotland. Sarah A., wife, 48 years, born Applecomb?
Berks. Children, George, 11 years. Sarah A., 9 years. Elizabeth,
4 years. Isabella, 2 years, all born Scotland.

DUNCAN William, marriedm 56 years, stonemason, born Scotland.
Living at High Street, Stokesley, North Riding of Yorkshire.
1881 census. With Mary A., wife, 54 years. Mary A. TIPLING,
dau., married, 19 years. James, son, 17 years, painter. Hannah,
dau., 14 years. Thomas, son, 10 years, all born Stokesley.

DYSON living at 4 Bridge Lane, Caldergate, Carlisle. 1851
census, Trinity. Thomas Dyson, married, 79 years, farmer, 14
acres, born Westward, Cmb. Dorothy, wife, 72 years, born Brough,
Cmb. Dorothy CRANMER, grand-dau., 19 years, born Carlisle. Sarah
CRANMER, grand-dau., 14 years, born Carlisle. William T.
CRANMER, grandson, 8 years, born Scotland. Folio 370.

EASTON Andrew, married, 45 years, sawyer, born Scotland. Living
at Chapel Buildings, Newcastle upon Tyne. 1871 census East All
Saints. With Agnes, wife, 44 years, born Scotland. Children,
Mary, 11 years, born South Shields. Christiana, 10 years, born
Hull, Yorkshire. Andrew James, 7 years, born Newcastle upon
Tyne.

EDGAR Robert, unmarried, 20 years, weaver, born Scotland.
Lodging in house of Sibby NOWELL, widow. 6 Bridge Lane,
Carlisle. 1851 census.

ELDER Archibald, unmarried, 28 years, weaver, born Scotland.
Lodging at house of Isaac TURNER. Parkham Beck, Carlisle. 1851
census.

ENGLISH Andrew, married, 26 years, blacksmith, born Scotland.
Living at 18 Chapel Buildings, Newcastle upon Tyne. 1871 census,
East All Saints. With Margaret Ann, wife, 30 years, born
Gateshead. Mary Elizabeth, dau., 2 years, born Newcastle upon
Tyne.

ENNIS Mowbrey, wife of William GUN, see GUN Isabella for
details.

ENNIS Peter, married, 65 years, Chelsea Pen., born Scotland.
Living at 49 Denton Holme, Carlisle. 1851 census. With Margaret,
wife, 60 years, born at Inthington, Cmb.

ENNES Mowbrey, born 29th November 1802, baptised 30th January
1803, 1st dau. of James Ennes, baker, native of Scotland, by his
wife Rachael UMPLEBY, native of Yorkshire. St. Hilda's, South
Shields, Co Durham, baptisms.

EWART James, unmarried, 19 years, baker, born Scotland. Lodging
at house of Hannah BENSON, grocer. 160 Church Street, Carlisle.
1851 census.

FAULS David, unmarried, 22 years, sailor, born Scotland. Lodging
in house of William NIMONS. 218 Pattinson Lane, Carlisle. 1851
census.

FLANAGAN John, married, 28 years, gingham weaver, born Scotland.
Living at 59 Bridge Lane, Carlisle. 1851 census. With Cath.,
wife, 27 years. Children, Bridget, 6 years. James, 1 year. John,
2 weeks, all born Carlisle.

FLECK Mary, born 22nd January 1803, baptised 20th March 1803,
2nd dau. of Ralph Fleck, joiner, native of North Britain, by his
wife, Elizabeth WHINHAM, native of Northumberland. St. Hilda's,
South Shields, baptisms.

FORBES William G. unmarried, 34 years, G.P. medicine, born
Scotland. 1881 census, Stokesley, North Riding of Yorkshire.

FORREST living at Old Road, Grappenhall, Warrington. 1851
census. David Forrest, 28 years, B--- Maker, born Scotland.
Elizabeth, 27 years, wife, born Appleton, Cheshire. Margaret,
dau., 6 years, born Latchford. Mary Forrest, 60 years, widow,
lodger, born Scotland. Mich. Forrest, 23 years, lodger, born
Scotland. Maria Forrest, 16 years, lodger, born Latchford.

FORREST John, widower, 51 years, warden of industrial school,
born Scotland. Garth Heads Ragged and Industrial School,
Newcastle-u-Tyne. 1871 census, East All Saints.

FORSYTH living at 121 Denton Hill, Carlisle. 1851 census. Jane
Forsyth, married, 46 years, housekeeper. John, son unmarried, 19
years, servant. Margaret, grand dau., 1 year. Jane Beatty, dau.,
17 years, servant. All born Scotland.

FORSYTH Andrew, native of Scotland, died Liverpool 5th December
1839 age 36 years. St. James, Liverpool, the Necropolis.

FOSTER William, widower, 61 years, pawnbroker, born Scotland.
Living at 81 Longmillgate, Manchester. 1851 census. With Hannah,
36 years, dau., born Halifax. James, 32 years, son, born
Halifax. Reel 2229 187a.

FRAISER John, 15 years, weaver, born Scotland. Visitor in house
of Thomas HUNTINGTON. 223 Parkam Beck, Carlisle. 1851 census.
(see same).

FRANKS Elizabeth, widow, 50 years, tailoress, born Scotland.
Visitor in house of George MAIN, 19 Buxton Street, Newcastle
upon Tyne. 1871 Census. (see same).

FRAZER Alexander, agent of Tudwick Farmhouse, a native of
Scotland, died of decay of nature. No. 3690, buried 30th August
1843, ward N, No. 216, depth 5 feet, age 74 years. Westgate
Cemetery, Newcastle upon Tyne.

FRENCH Alex., married, 61 years, farm steward, born Scotland.
Living at Rushen, 1851 census, Isle of Man. With Margaret, wife,
63 years. Margaret, dau., unmarried, 27 years, dressmaker.
Richard, grandson, 5 years. Margaret, grand dau., 2 years, all
born Rushen, Isle of Man. Book 1, page 38, entry 128, Kentraugh.
From Isle of Man FHS.

GAMBLES Mary, unmarried, 19 years, born Scotland. Visitor in
house of Mary CONNOLLY. 15 Blue Anchor Lane, Caldergate,
Carlisle. 1851 census, Trinity page 1.

GARVENLOOK Robert, 9 years, relative of Andrew H. LAW. see LAW
for details.

GAW Robert, son in law of Joseph ALLEN, 41 years, hand loom
weaver, born Scotland. Living with father in law at 21 John
Street, Bolton. 1851 census. Also Mary Gaw, wife, 41 years,
Bettsy his dau., 4 year, all born Bolton. Details of his wifes
family are - Joseph ALLEN, 64 years, hand loom weaver, born
Bedford. Ellen, wife, 64 years. Joseph, son, 25 years, all born
Bolton. Reel 14, 2211 Id folio 142a.

GEDDES Andrew, 52 years, widower, wireworker, born Scotland.
Living at John Street, Warrington. 1851 census. With children,
William, 23 years, druggist. Sarah, 19 years. George, 10 years,
Mary, 7 years. All born Warrington.

GEDDES John, 54 years, tea dealer, born Scotland. Living at
Bewsey Street, Warrington. 1851 census. With Amelia, wife, 51
years? born Keswick?

GIBSON David, married, 32 years, carpenter, born Scotland. Living at 171 Murrell Hill, Carlisle. 1851 census. With Ann, wife, 22 years, born Crosscandbie? Cmb. Jane, dau., 7 months, born Carlisle.

GIBSON Robert, married, 32 years, tailor, born Scotland. Living at Stokesley, North Riding of Yorkshire. 1881 census. With Margaret, wife, 27 years, born Stokesley.

GILBERTSON Elizabeth, 22 years, born Scotland. Lodger in house of William Gilbertson. 144 Cobden Street, Carlisle. 1851 census.

GILCHRIST John, married, 70 years, draper, born Scotland. Living at Stokesley, North Riding of Yorkshire. 1881 census. With Sophia, wife, 62 years, born Stokesley.

GILLIES John, 37 years, bookbinder finisher, born Scotland. Living at 44 Union Terrace, St, Giles, Yorkshire. 1851 census. With Elizabeth, 29 years, wife, born York. Clara Jane, dau., under 1 month, born St. Giles.

GLASS? GLUSS? or GLATS Andrew, unmarried, 27 years, farm bailiff, born Scotland. Living at 63 Plainfield Farm House. 1851 census, Poole area, Dorset.

GLENDINNING William, 52 years, horse? or house tenter, born Scotland. Living at Heath Lane, Warrington, 1851 census. With Mary, wife, 46 years? born Lune? Cumberland. Children, John, 13 years. Thomas, 11 years. Richard, 9 years. Elizabeth, 7 years. All born Warrington.

GLENDINNING John, married, 25 years, weaver, born Scotland. Living at 43 Byron Street, Carlisle. 1851 census. With Eliza, wife, 28 years, born Ireland. Mary, dau., 9 years, born Scotland. Elizabeth, dau., 3 years, born Carlisle.

GLOAG or CLOAG?? see CLOAG? John for details.

GLOVER Sarah, unmarried, 28 years, born Scotland. Visitor in house of John WALLACE (see same). 25 Gaythrops Lane, Carlisle. 1851 census.

GLOVER Sally, unmarried, 28 years, servant, born Scotland. Visitor in house of Hugh McDERMOT. 12 Gaythrops Lane, Carlisle. 1851 census.

GORDON Daniel, 50 years, labourer, born Scotland. Living at Queen Street, Bolton. 1841 census.

GORDON living at 13 Bridge Lane, Carlisle. 1851 census. Jane Gordon, head, married, 46 years, winder. Children, Robert, unmarried, 23 years, rail lab. Adam, 17 years, rail lab. all born Scotland. John, 9 years, born Carlisle. Walter, 7 years, born Scotland.

GRAHAM Wiliam, married, 25 years, shoemaker, born Scotland.
Living at 22 Blagdon Street, Newcastle upon Tyne. 1871 census,
East All Saints. With Agnes, wife, 32 years, born Newcastle.

GRAHAM Mary, unmarried, 27 years, work marine stores, born
Scotland. Living at 64 Bridge Lane, Carlisle. 1851 census. With
Jane, dau., 4 years, Mary Ann, dau., 2 years, both born
Carlisle.

GRAHAM Irving, 21 years, servant miller, born Scotland. Living
in house of Joseph ROBINSON, miller. 128 Denton Hill, Carlisle.
1851 census.

GRAHAM living at 206 Pattinson Lane, Carlisle. 1851 census.
Irving Graham, married, 58, miller, born Westward, Cmb. Agnes,
wife, 57 years. Children, Isaac, unmarried, 30 years, miller.
Jane, unmarried, 20 years. Catherine, 18 years, dressmaker.
John, 16 years. Sarah, 12 years. William, 7 years, all born
Scotland. See previous entry.

GRAHAM James, married, 51 years, weaver, born Scotland. Living
at Caldcoats, Carlisle. 1851 census. With Ann, wife, 38 years,
born Carlisle. Children, Jane, 17 years. Agness, 15 years.
Margaret, 6 years. Ann, 2 years, all born Cumbria.

GRAHAM living at 183 Denton Holme Head, Carlisle. 1851 census.
John Graham, married, 47 years, warehouseman. Mary, wife, 40
years, both born Ireland. Children, Henry, 21 years, unmarried,
weaver. Thomas, 18 years, warehouseman. Margaret, 8 years, all
born Scotland. William, 4 years, born Carlisle. Caldergate,
Trinity, page 42, folio 390.

GRANT George A. married, 34 years, print compositor, born
Scotland. Living at 50 Gibson Street, Newcastle upon Tyne. 1871
census, East All Saints. With Margaret, wife, 32 years.
Children, Jane Ann, 9 years. Isabella, 2 years. Mary, 1 month,
all born Newcastle.

GRAY William, married, 28 years, master rigger, born Scotland.
Living at 192 West Quay, Poole, Dorset. With, Sarah, wife, 29
years, born Swanage, Dorset. Mary ORMOND, 9 years, dau. of wife,
born Swanage, Dorset. Ester F. Gray, dau., 1 year, born Poole,
Dorset. Reel HO 107. 1851 census.

GRAY Lewis, married, 38 years, licensed victualler, born
Scotland. Living at White Hart Inn, Dolphin Lane, Dover, Kent.
1871 census. With Harriet, wife, 40 years, born Sittingbourne,
Kent. Children, Hannicy?, son, 14 years, born Canterbury, Kent.
Thomas, 12 years, born St. Margarets, Kent. Lewis, 10 years,
born Jersey. Mary Ann RENSHAW, unmarried, sister, 36 years, born
Sittingbourne, Kent. Reel 10/1007.

GREAVES Jane and Robert, step children of William HUDSON, see
HUDSON for details.

GREGSON Ellen, 61 years, unmarried, tailoress, born Scotland.
Lodging in house of George MAIN. 19 Buxton Street, Newcastle
upon tyne. 1871 census, East All Saints.

GREY Ann born 9th May 1804, baptised 1st June 1804, 2nd dau. of
James Grey, mariner, native of North Britain, by his wife Hannah
WILBERFORCE, native of this place. St. Hilda's, South Shields,
Co Durham, baptisms.

GRIERSON living at 32 Newtown, Whitehaven, 1851 census, Holy
Trinity. Jos. Grierson, 40 years, stonemason, born Scotland.
Ann, wife, 39 years, born Whitehaven. Children, Mary, 14 years,
born Carlisle. Robert, 12 years, born Scotland. Jane Ann
GRIERSTON! dau., 7 years. Dinah Ed., 4 years. Robina, 1 year,
all born Whitehaven.

GRIEVES John, married, 24 years, weaver, born Scotland. Living
at 219 Parkam Beck, Carlisle. 1851 census, Carlisle. With Ann,
wife, 26 years. Thomas, son, 6 years. Mary, dau., 2 years, all
born Carlisle.

GRIEVES Thomas, married, 28 years, weaver, born Scotland. Living
at 62 Byron Street, Carlisle. 1851 census, Caldergate Trinity.
Folio 313. With Ellen, wife, 32 years, weaver, born Scotland.

GRIGG John, 24 years, glass makers labourer, born Scotland.
Living at Eccleston Street, Eccleston, St. Helens, Lancs. 1851
Census. With Margaret, wife, 21 years, born Scotland. Sarah,
dau., 1 year, born St. Helens, Lancs.

GUN Isabella, born 21st January 1803, baptised 1st June 1803,
3rd sau. of William Gun, carpenter, native of North Britain, by
his wife Mowbrey ENNIS, native of North Britain. St. Hilda's,
South Shields, Co Durham, baptisms.

GUNN Alexander, born 6th November 1804, baptised 3rd March 1805,
3rd son of Alexander Gunn, bottlemaker, native of North Britain,
by his wife Jane STOKEL? native of Sunderland. St. Hilda's,
South Shields, Co Durham, baptisms.

HAFFIN James, widower, 78 years, labourer, born Scotland.
Lodging in house of Joseph NIXON. Cobden Street, Carlisle. 1851
census.

HAMILTON living at 26 Chapel Buildings, Newcastle upon Tyne.
1871 census, East All Saints. William Hamilton, 31 years,
tailor, born North Shields. Elizabeth, wife, 32 years, born
Newcastle. Children, Matthew, 8 years. William, 7 years, both
born Newcastle. George, 3 years. Robert, 1 year, both born
Scotland.

HAMILTON living at 141 Denton Hill, Carlisle. 1851 census. John
Hamilton, married, 36 years, dyer. Hannah, wife, 39 years.
Jessie, dau., 8 years, all born Scotland. Hannah, dau., 5 years.
John, son, 1 year, both born Carlisle.

HANDYSIDE John Hepburn, married, 37 years, gen. pract.
L.R.C.S.E. born Scotland. Living at Stokesley, North Riding of
Yorkshire. 1881 census. With Hannah, 45 years, born Stokesley.

HANNAY living at 42 Thomas Street, St. Pauls, Manchester. 1851
census. John Hannay, 50 years, draper. Margaret, wife, 43 years,
both born Scotland. Mary Ellen, dau., 11 years. James, son, 9
years, both born Manchester. David, brother, 29 years,
unmarried, draper, born Scotland. Reel 2229.

HARRIS living at Caldcoats, Carlisle. 1851 census. William
Harris, married, 44 years, weaver. Mary, wife, 41 years, winder.
Children, Janet, 14 years, weaver. Margaret, 17? years. Mary, 10
years. Andrew, 5 years, all born Scotland. William, 1 year, born
Carlisle.

HASTINGS Alexander, married, 25 years, plumber, born Scotland.
Living at 45 Melbourne Street, Newcastle upon Tyne. 1871 census,
East All Saints. With Mary Ann, wife, 25 years. Thomas, son, 3
years. Alexander, son, 1 year, all born Gateshead, Durham.

HAY living at Lever Lane, Little Lever, Bolton. 1851 census.
William Hay, 30 years, joiner. Hannah, wife, 30 years. Children,
Mary, 9 years. John, 7 years. Isabella, 3 years, all born
Scotland. Reel 14 2211, 2Cd, folio 613a.

HAY William, married, 40 years, carter, born Scotland. Living at
33 Industrial Dwellings, Newcastle upon Tyne. 1871 census. East
All Saints. With Mary, wife, 36 years, born Scotland.

HAY Peter, married, 34 years, farm bailiff, born Scotland.
Living at 95 Newtown Farm, Poole area, Dorset. 1851 census. With
Emily, wife, 26 years, born Whaddon, Bucks. Peter, son, 3 years.
Emily, dau., 1 year, both born Dorset.

HAY James, unmarried, 23 years, baker, born Scotland. Lodging
with Alex. McTURK (see same), 179 Church Street, Carlisle. 1851
census.

HENDERSON living at 17 Chapel Buildings, Newcastle upon Tyne.
1871 census, East All Saints. Thomas Henderson, 32 years, seaman
(Royal Naval Reserve). Isabella, wife, 35 years. Children,
Thomas, 6 years. William Gordon, 3 years. Isabella, 10 months,
all born Scotland.

HENDERSON John James, unmarried, 18 years, groom, born Scotland.
Living at Stokesley, North Riding of Yorkshire. 1881 census.

HENDERSON living at Stokesley, North Riding of Yorkshire. Andrew
Henderson, married, 50 years, groom. Margaret, wife, 49 years,
both born Scotland. Children, Peter D. unmarried, 22 years,
cabinet maker unemployed, born Liverpool, Lancs. George, 14
years, gardener. Margaret, 12 years, both born Scotland. See
previous entry.

HENRY living at 4 Victoria Place, Newcastle upon Tyne. 1871
census, East All Saints. Annie Henry, married, 39 years,
seaman's wife. Children, Annie, 16 years, dressmaker. Thomas I.
14 years, clerk. Robert M. 9 years. James, 7 years, all born
Scotland.

HEPPEL John, married, 61 years, shoemaker, born Scotland. Living
at 20 Chapel Buildings, Newcastle upon Tyne. 1871 census, East
All Saints. With Catherine, wife, 60 years, shoemaker, born
Blaydon, Northumberland. Margaret ROW, granddau., 8 years. Henny
ROW, granddau., 1 year, both born Newcastle.

HESLOP living at 19 Blagdon Street, Newcastle upon Tyne. 1871
census, East All Saints. Alexander Heslop, married, 32 years,
tailor. Agnes, wife, 30 years. William, son, 12 years. Jessie,
dau., 10 years, all born Scotland.

HILL Walter, married, 35 years, warper, born Scotland. Living at
35 Byron Street, Carlisle. 1851 census. With Ann, wife, 45
years. Edw., son, 8 years, both born Carlisle.

HOOLSHAM living at 60 Bridge Lane, Carlisle. 1851 census. Hugh
Hoolsham, married, 45 years, Chelsea Pen., born Ireland. Mary,
wife, 43 years, washerwoman, born Carlisle. Children, John, 19
years, weaver, born Scotland. William, 18 years, born Ireland.
Hugh, 14 years, born Malta. Thomas, 11 years. Margaret, 8 years.
Jane, 4 years, all born Carlisle.

HUDSON living at Caldcoats, Carlisle. 1851 census. William
Hudson, married, 77 years, tailor, born Carlisle. Margaret,
wife, 53 years, born Scotland. Jane GREAVES, step-dau., 19
years, weaver. Robert GREAVES, step-son, 15 years, weaver, both
born Scotland.

HULL living at Caldcoats, Carlisle, 1851 census. Mary Hull,
married, 34 years, winder. Robert, son, 13 years, weaver.
Jessie, dau., 5 years, all born Scotland.

HUNT Edward, married, 38 years, bricklayer and lodging house
keeper, born Scotland. Living at 16 Blue Anchor Lane, Carlisle.
1851 census. With Mary, wife, 37 years. Patrick, son, 14 years.
Thomas MANUS, visitor, unmarried, 30 years, labourer. Patrick
RYLEY, unmarried, visitor, hawker of smallware, all born
Scotland.

HUNTER Catherine, born 8th September 1803, baptised 7th February
1804, 4th dau. of John Hunter, native of this place, by his wife
Catherine MUIR, native of North Britain. St. Hilda's, South
Shields, Co Durham, baptisms.

HUNTINGTON living at 223 Parkam Beck, Carlisle. 1851 census.
Thomas Huntington, married, 25 years, printworks, born Wigton.
Eliza, wife, 22 years, born Scotland. Ann, dau., 2 months, born
Carlisle. John FRAISER, visitor, 15 years, weaver, born
Scotland.

HUTCHINSON Daniel, married, 32 years, rail lab., born Scotland.
Living at 79 Byron Street, Carlisle. 1851 census. With Hannah,
wife, 28 years. Children, Thomas S. 8 years. Ann, 5 years. Jane,
2 years, all born Carlisle.

IMERY William, 37? years, head gardener, born Scotland. Living
at Goosnargh Lodge Cottage, Goosnargh, Lancs. 1851 census. With
Martha, wife, 32 years, born Winkfield? Berks.

IRVING James, unmarried, 26 years, biscuit maker, born Scotland.
Lodging at house of Mary BOROMAN. 126 Bread Street, Carlisle.
1851 census.

IRVING George, widower, 49 years, labourer, born Scotland.
Living at 118 Denton Hill, Carlisle. 1851 census. With Margaret,
dau., 20 years, housekeeper, born Rockcliff, Cmb. John, son, 18
years, dyer, born Kirkhinton, Cmb. Joseph, son, 16 years, born
Carlisle.

IRVING Richard, married, 48 years, shipwright, born Scotland.
Living at Cobden Street, Carlisle. 1851 census. With Ellen,
wife, 45 years, born Scotland. Children, Margaret, 10 years.
John, 8 years. Andrew, 2 years, all born Carlisle.

IRVING George, married, 47 years, shipsmaster, born Scotland.
Lodging at Caldcoats, Carlisle. 1851 census. With Mary, wife, 40
years, born Harrington, Cmb. Children, James, 12 years. John, 10
years. Joseph, 8 years, all born Whitehaven. William, 5 years.
George, 2 months, both born Bowness.

IRVING David, married, 35 years, shoemaker, born Scotland.
Living at 24 Chambers Court, Carlisle. 1851 census. With Mary,
wife, 35 years, shoe binder, born Cumwhinton, Cmb. Children,
Sushanna, 14 years, born Carlisle. David S. 12 years, born
Newcastle. Thomas, 10 years. William, 6 years. Margaret D. 1
year, all born Carlisle.

JACKSON Mary, unmarried, 30 years, house servant, born Scotland.
Servant to Thomas NELSON (see same) 169 Murrell Hill, Carlisle.
1851 census.

JAMUSON Phillip, 38 years, gas meter maker, born Scotland.
Living at 18 Partridge Street, Bolton. 1861 census. With
Elizabeth, wife, 40 years, born Shropshire Hall, Brighton.
Children, Margaret, 11 years. David, 8 years. James, 10 months,
all born Bolton, Lancs.

JOFS? or JOJO? William, 39 years, Chelsea Pensioner, born
Scotland. Living at Dover, St. James, 1861 census. With
Elizabeth, 28 years, born St. Margarets at Cliffe, Kent. Reel
9/548.

JOHNSTON John, married, 70 years, joiner, born Scotland. Living
at 142 Bread Street, Carlisle. 1851 census. With Mary, wife, 50
years. Mary, granddau., 10 years, both born Carlisle.

JOHNSTON Isabella, unmarried, 17 years, born Scotland. Servant in house of George STORDY, Inn keeper. Caldcoats, Carlisle, 1851 census.

JOHNSTON John, married, 26 years, seaman, born Scotland. Living at Caldcoats, Carlisle. 1851 census. With Frances, wife, 25 years. Children, Mary, 1 year! William, 9 months! all born Carlisle.

JOHNSTON Robert, widower, 64 years, book keeper - warehouse, born Scotland. Living at 68 Stock Street, St. Thomas, Manchester. 1851 census. With Sarah Ann WHITE, dau., widow, born Hulme. John Henry White, 12 years, grandson, born Ardwick. Robert N. White, 10 years, grandson. Annie White, 4 years, granddau., both born Manchester. Reel 2229.

JOHNSTONE Robert, born 1818. In 1851 and 1861 census, living at Churcham, Gloucester. In 1871 census, living at Newtown, Gloucester, born Scotland.

KEACHER William, married, 35 years, coastguard, born Scotland. Living at 38 East Cliffe, Guston, Dover. 1871 census. With Caroline, wife, 32 years, born Portsea, Hants. Children, John J. 8 years, born Portsea. Caroline C. 2 years. George, 1 month, both born Guston, Kent. Reel RG 10/1008.

KEAY living at Red Bank, St. Thomas, Manchester. 1851 census. John Keay, 34 years, joiner. Eliz., wife, 32 years. James, son, 11 years. Eliz., dau., 9 years, all born Scotland. Reel 2229.

KEITLEY? James, 11 years, scholar, born Scotland. Inmate of Garth Heads Ragged and Industrial Schools, Newcastle upon Tyne. 1871 census, East All Saints.

KELLY living at Eccleston Street, Eccleston, St. Helens, Lancs. 1851 census. James Kelly, 44 years, glass maker. Margaret, wife, 40 years, both born Ireland. Children, Margaret, 22 years. Peter, 20 years, glass maker. Daniel, 14 years, glass maker. John, 12 years, glass maker. Mary A. 9 years. Nathan, 6 years. Elizabeth, 4 years. James BROSS, grandson, 7? years, all born Scotland.

KERR Andrew, married, 31 years, brewer, born Scotland. Living at 94 Denton Holme, Carlisle. 1851 census. With Eliz., wife, 32 years, born Scotland.

KERR William, unmarried, 24 years, pianoforte maker, born Scotland, N.K. Visitor in house of Mr. WILLIS, 54 Longfleet, Poole area, Dorset. 1851 census.

KEY living at 136 Wimborne Road, Poole area, Dorset. 1851 census. Thomas Key, married, 46 years, surveyer inland revenue. Agnes, wife, 35 years. Children, Isabella, 13 years. John, 10 years. Thomas, 9 years. William, 7 years. Barbara, 5 years, all born Scotland. Agnes, 2 years. James, 2 months, both born Longfleet, Dorset.

KILLPATRICK George, married, 50 years, L H weaver cotton, born
Scotland. Living at 88 Bridge Lane, Carlisle. Caldergate
Trinity, 1851 census. With Mary, wife, 44 years, born
Birmingham. Children, Thomas, 19 years. Mary, 16 years.
Margaret, 13 years. John, 8 years. George, 5 years, Alexander, 2
years, all born Carlisle. Page 24, folio 348.

KIRKPATRICK James, 52 years, beerhouse keeper, born Scotland.
Living at 18 Brown Street, St. Ann's, Manchester. 1851 census.
With Ann, Wife, 54 years, born Manchester. Janet, dau., 23
years, born Manchester. Reel 2229.

KIRKPATRICK James, married, 78 years, labourer pauper weaver,
born Scotland. Living at 76 Bridge Lane, Carlisle. 1851 census.

KIRKWOOD John, 25 years, coastguard, born Scotland. Living at
Dolphin Street, Deal, Kent. 1841 census. With Harriot, 25 years,
not born in Kent. Harriot, 6 months, born in Kent. Reel
RG107/466.

LAMONT living at 166 Church Street, Carlisle. 1851 census. Peter
Lamont, married, 31 years, baker. Margaret, wife, 32 years.
William, son, 13 years, all born Scotland. John, son, 2 years,
born Cmb. county.

LAW living at Burnden, Bolton. 1851 census. Andrew H. Law, 25
years, joiner. Jane, wife, 29 years, both born Scotland. John,
son, 3 months, born Great Lever, Bolton. Robert GARVENLOOK,
relative, 9 years, born Scotland. Reel 2211, Ib, folio 543a.

LEECH Ann, born 10th May 1812, baptised 29th May 1812, 1st dau.
of James Leech, militia man, native of North Britain, by his
wife, Elizabeth, dau. of John HALL, native of this Chapelry. St.
John's, Newcastle upon Tyne, baptisms.

LEIGHTON Andrew Sinclair, 35 years, steward Liverpool Exchange
Club, born Scotland. Living at Chorley and Dist. Lancs. (town),
1851 census. Reel 2263, folio 025.

LINDSAY Peter, 80 years, draper, born Scotland. Living at 37
Bradford Road, St. Phillips, Manchester. 1851 census. With
Elizabeth, wife, 74 years, born Marple, Cheshire. Reel HO
107/2226, page 791a.

LOGAN John, 47 years, married, land agent, born Scotland. Living
at Barton Cottage, Barton St. Laurence, North Lancs. 1851
census. With Margaret Corner, dau., 4 years. Janet Gibson, dau.,
2 years. George, son, 1 year, all born Barton, Lancs.

LOMTHEITES? Jane, unmarried, 24 years, born Scotland. Servant in
house of Jane McCORMICK, married, 44 years, charwoman, born
Scotland. 91 Denton Holme, Carlisle. 1851 census.

LOVE Murray, 30 years, coastgaurd, born Scotland. Living at Kingsgate, St. Peters, Thanet, Kent. 1841 census. With Jane, 30 years, born Scotland. Murray, 6 years, born in Kent. Jane, 10 years, born Scotland. Ann, 8 years, born Scotland. Isabell, 4 years, born Kent. Esther, 1 year, born Kent. Reel HO 107/468.

LUNT Mary wife of Captain William Lunt, 93rd Highlanders, died 11th June 1835 age 69 years. Captain William Lunt her husband, died 23rd June 1843 age 71 years. St. James, Liverpool, the Necropolis, nonconformists.

LYALL Smith, 30 years, millwright, born Scotland. Living at 14 Marcer? Street, St. Phillips, Manchester. 1851 census. With Elizabeth, 26 years, wife, born Scotland. Aaron, son, 5 years. William, son, 8 months, both born Manchester. Margaret GIBSON, 14 years, dau. in law! born Scotland. Reel HO 107/2226 p. 760a.

MACK Thomas, 53 years, shuttle maker, born Scotland. Living at 158 Murrell Hill, Carlisle. 1851 census. With Sarah, wife, 48 years. Children, Margaret, 19 years, machine girl. Isabella, 11 years. Elizabeth, 9 years, all born Scotland.

MAIN living at 19 Buxton Street, Newcastle upon Tyne. 1871 census, East All Saints. George Main, married, 52 years, fishmonger. Mary, wife, 52 years. Children, John, unmarried, 20 years, barber. Isabella, unmarried, 24 years, all born Scotland. Mary, 17 years, born Newcastle.

MANUS Thomas, visitor in house of Edward HUNT, see same for details.

MARSHALL William, married, 32 years, horn? manufacturer, born Scotland. Lodging in house of Patrick MOONEY. 55 Bridge Street, Carlisle. 1851 census.

MASTERMAN Henry, 11 years, scholar, born Scotland. Inmate of Garth Heads Ragged and Industrial Schools, Newcastle upon Tyne. 1871 census, East All Saints.

MAXWELL Mary, unmarried, 40 years, house servant, born Scotland. Chorley and Dist., Lancs. (town). 1851 census. Reel 2263 folio 008.

MEAD Ellen, 11 years, scholar, born Scotland. Glossop Convent, Church Street, Glossop, Cheshire. 1871 census.

MERCIER, Sarah, 9 years, dau., born Scotland. St. Philip, Birmingham, 1851 census. En. 14, sch. 1.

MERITON William, unmarried, 36 years, railway labourer, born Scotland. Lodging at Park Street, Hatfield Herts. 1851 census. Reel HO 107/1712, p. 5, folio 120, sch. 21.

MILLER William, married, 47 yrs. confectioner, born Scotland. Living at 33 Melbourne St. Newcastle-u-Tyne. 1871 census, East All Saints. With Isabella, wife, 40 yrs. born north Sunderland. Children, Isabella, 14 yrs. born Scotland. William, son, born

Morpeth. Janet, 10 years, born Scotland. John, 7 years. Elisie,
4 years. Ellen, 2 years, all born Newcastle.

MILLICAN living at Parkham Beck, Carlisle. 1851 census. William
Millican, married, 52 years, weaver, born Scotland. Ann, wife,
38 years, weaver, born Carlisle. Children, William, 17 years,
weaver, born Scotland. Richard, 10 years. Margaret, 6 years.
Edmond, 5 years. Benjamin, 9 months, all born Caldecoats,
Carlisle.

MITCHELL John, 63 years, under factory manager, born Scotland.
Living at 20 Ancoats Grove, All Souls, Manchester. 1851 census.
With Mary, wife, 59 years, born Ashton under Lyne, Lancs. Sarah,
dau., 29 years. Alex. George, son, 20 years. Alfred Mitchell
DOBSON, 9 years, grandson, all born Manchester. Reel HO
107/2226, page 675.

MOFFAT Corbatt, 42 years, weaver, born Scotland. Lodging in
house of James RUSSELL (listed in 1st section of dictionary). 5
Bengal Square, Bolton. 1851 census. Reel 2211 Ig, folio 214.

MOFFAT living at 116 Jane or June Street, Carlisle. 1851 census.
Mary Moffat, widow, 45 years, bobbin w. born Ireland. Children,
Jannet, 9 years. Mary, 7 years. Jane, 5 years, all born
Scotland. Andrew, 2 years. James, 6 months, both born Carlisle.
Catherine DIMOND, sister, 25 years, born Ireland.

MOLLONS living at Caldcoats, Carlisle. 1851 census, Trinity.
George Mollons, married, 51 years, mariner. Martha, wife, 47
years. Mary ATKIN, dau., married, 23 years, all born Scotland.
John Atkin, grandson, 5 years. William Atkin, grandson, 3 years.
Charlotte Atkin, granddau., 7 months, all born Carlisle. Reel HO
107/2430. page 1, folio 272.

MONTGOMERY James, married, 46 years, rag enquirer, born
Scotland. Living at 63 Blossom Street, Ancoats, Manchester. 1881
census. With Mary, wife, 36 years, born Gloucester. Sarah, dau.,
7 years, born Somerset. Reel 2855, dist. 8.

MOORE Robert, married, 20 years, H. L. weaver, born Scotland.
Living at 105 Bridge Lane, Carlisle. 1851 census. With
Elizabeth, wife, 32 years, staymaker, born Scotland. Henry,
father, married, 58 years, weaver, born Ireland.

MORGAN Francis, married, 40 years, lithographer, born Scotland.
Lodging at house of John W. BIRMINGHAM. 4 Industrial Dwellings,
Newcastle upon Tyne. 1871 census, East All Saints.

MORRIS living at 12 Industrial Dwellings, Newcastle upon Tyne.
1871 census, East All Saints. Isabella Morris, married, seaman's
wife. John, son, unmarried, 21 years, painter. James, son, 15
years, labourer, all born Scotland.

MORRISON living at 24 Bridge Lane, Carlisle. 1851 census. James
Morrison, widower, 31 yrs. brewer. Children, Margaret, 20 yrs.
brewer. John, 16 yrs. Caroline Morrison, (not one of children),
servant, 16 yrs, all born Scotland.

MORROW Francis, widower, 66 years, H. L. weaver, born Scotland.
Living at 17 Blue Anchor Lane, Carlisle. 1851 census. With
Francis, son, married, 26 years, H. L. weaver, born Carlisle.
Ann, dau. in law, 28 years, bobbin winder, born Ireland. John,
grandson, 10 months, born Carlisle.

MORTON Joseph, 43 years, hand loom weaver, born Scotland. Living
at Chorley town, Lancs. 1851 census. With Sarah, wife, 41 years,
hand loom weaver, born Scotland. Reel 2263, folio 066.

MUIR living at 103 Bridge Lane, Carlisle. 1851 census. William
Muir, married, 45 years, A. L. weaver. Isabella, wife, 40 years.
Children, Janet, unmarried, 21 years, steam loom weaver. John,
19 years, weaver. Jane, 17 years, machine winder. James, 12
years. Isabella, 7 years, all born Scotland.

MUIR Catherine, wife of John HUNTER, see HUNTER Catherine for
details.

MUIR living at 187 Willow Holme, Carlisle. 1851 census. James
Muir, married, 38 years, warper and spinner. Agnes, wife, 40
years, washerwoman. Children, Thomas, 15 years, boiler
apprentice. John, 12 years, biscuit baker. Andrew, 10 years, all
born Scotland.

MULHOLLAND Alexander, married, 40 years, weaver, born Scotland.
Living at 192 Parkam Beck, Carlisle. 1851 census. With Mary,
wife, 38 years, born Sowerby. Children, Thomas, 16 years. Mary,
5 years. Jane, 1 year, all born Caldergate. Mary, mother, 68
years, born Ireland. Reel Caldergate, Trinity, folio 296, p. 50.

MUNRO George, married, 44 years, labourer, born Scotland. Living
at 11 Grass Street, Ancoats, Manchester. 1881 census. With Jane,
wife, 44 years, born Scotland. Alexander, son, 14 years, errand
boy, born Leeds. Reel 2855, dist. 9.

MURRAY George, 78 years, cotton spinner, born Scotland. Living
at 333 Gt. Ancoats Street, All Souls, Manchester. 1851 census.
With Jane, wife, 72 years, born Chowbent. James, son married, 46
years, born Manchester. Reel HO 107/2226 page 658a.

MURRAY Elizabeth B. born Scotland, sister in law of Thomas FOX.
Living at South Street, Bingley, Keighley, Yorkshire. 1861
census.

MURRAY living at Caldcoats, Carlisle. 1851 census. James Murray,
married, 60 years, gardener. Mary, wife, 55 years. Children,
Sarah, 27 years, unmarried, cook. David, 18 years, plate layer.
James, 16 years, blacksmith. Charles, 14 years, labourer.
Daniel, 12 years. William, 5 years, all born Scotland.
Elizabeth, 7 years, born Cumberland. Mary, granddau., 9 months,
born Carlisle.

MURRAY John, married, 43 yrs. warehouseman, born Scotland.
Living at 26 Chapel Buildings, Newcastle-u-Tyne. 1871 census,
East All Saints. With Ann, wife, 38 yrs. Children, Annie, 10 yrs
William, 8 yrs. John, 6 yrs. Euphemia, 2 yrs, all born Northd.

MURRAY William, 18 years, grocers porter, born Scotland. Lodging
in house of Patrick O'CONNAL. 48 Bridge Street, Carlisle. 1851
census.

MUVATT? Thomas, unmarried, 21 years, baker, born Scotland.
Visitor in house of Jos. HARRISON. 124 Watson Court, Carlisle.
1851 census.

McALLISTER Joseph, widower, 68 years, born Scotland. Father in
law of Thomas ROBERTS, born Carlisle. 173 Chappel Lane,
Carlisle. 1851 census.

McAVOY living at 2 Grenville Street, Newcastle upon Tyne. 1871
census, East All Saints. John McAvoy, married, 38 years,
grinder? in factory. Sarah, wife, 39 years, works in rope works,
both born Ireland. John, son, 13 years, imbecile since birth,
born Scotland.

McCALLEY? John, unmarried, 18 years, glass maker, born Scotland.
Lodging at Eccleston Street, Eccleston, St Helens, Lancs. 1851
census.

McCLAEN James, married, 34 years, born Scotland. Living at 38
Denton Holme, Carlisle. 1851 census. With Mary, wife, 34 years.
Children, David, 10 years. John, 5 years. Mary, 1 year, all born
Carlisle.

McCLINTON Andrew, 48 years, spinner, born Scotland. Living at 6
Garden Street, St. Andrew, Manchester. 1851 census. With
Isabella, 46 years, wife. Mary Jane, dau., 22 years, both born
Scotland. Elizabeth, dau., 16 years. Archibald, 12 years.
Robert, 9 years, all born Manchester. Reel HO 107/2226 p. 709a.

McCOLL Angus, of full age, engineer, born Scotland, father Hugh
McColl, farmer. Married Margaret WARNOCK, of full age, born
Scotland, father Robert Warnock, labourer. At St. John's Church,
Pembroke Dock, by license, 25th August 1843. See next entry.

McCOLL living at Laws Street South, Pembroke Dock. 1881 census.
Angus McColl, married, 50 years, foreman of engineers. Margaret,
wife, 45 years, foreman's wife. Hugh, son, unmarried, 23 years,
engine fitter, all born Scotland. Helen W. dau., 16 years, appr.
milliner. Jessie R. dau., 14 years. Marion W. dau., 12 years.
Margaret J. dau., 9 years. Robert J. son, 6 years, all born
Pembroke Dock. See previous entry for marriage.

McCORD living at 1 Walkers Building, Whitehaven. 1851 census,
Holy Trinity. Daniel McCord, 39 years, coalminer. Ellen, wife,
34 years, both born Scotland. John, son, 2 years, born
Whitehaven. John, brother, unmarried, 37 years, shoemaker.
Patrick, brother, 28 years, blacksmith. Henry FITZSIMMONS,
visitor, 18 years, ships carpenter, all born Scotland.

McCOWELL John, 57 years, insurance agent, born Scotland. Living at 19 Greenhalgh Street, Bolton. 1881 census. With Sarah, wife, 38 years, born Abergaveny, Monmouthshire. Children, Jane, 14 years, cotton tenter unemployed. Laura, 13 years, cotton tenter unemployed, both born Kirkheaton, Yorkshire. Hannah, 6 years. Eliza, 4 years. Henrietta, 4 months, all born Bolton. Reel 7, 3836, 19.

McCREAVEY Neil, married, 54 years, weaver, born Scotland. Living at Parkham Beck, Carlisle. 1851 census. With Margaret, wife, 38 years, born Carlisle. Children, Sarah, 30 years, weaver, born Cannomore, East Indies. Thomas, 17 years. Elizabeth, 15 years. Catherine, 13 years. Neil, 5 years. Mary, 3 years, all born Carlisle.

McCULLOCH James, married, 37 years, paper ruler, born Scotland. Living at 42 Industrial Dwellings, Newcastle upon Tyne. 1871 census, East All Saints. With Mary, wife, 28 years, born Scotland. Children, Alexander, 8 years. Margaret, 3 years. Alexandra, 1 year, all born Newcastle.

McDONALD John, born 17th December 1802, baptised 22nd May 1803, 1st son of David McDonald, mariner, native of North Britain, by his wife Ann BARRIN? native of Newcastle upon Tyne. St. Hilda's, South Shields, Co Durham, baptisms.

McDONALD John, 60 years, shoemaker, born Scotland. Living at 1 Gas Street, Lower King Street, Manchester. 1851 census. With Sarah, wife, 60 years, born Scotland. Sarah, dau., 21 years, born Manchester. Reel 2229.

McDONALD Hugh, 26 years, unmarried, railway labourer, born Scotland. Lodging at Park Street, Hatfield, Herts. 1851 census. Reel HO 107/1712, p. 5, folio 120, sch. 21.

McDOUGALL Angus, 47 years, master cooper employing 5 men, born Scotland. Living at 3 Hardy Street, Township of Eccleston, St. Helens, Lancs. 1851 census. With Catherine, wife, 53 years, housekeeper, born Scotland. Allen McLEOD, nephew, 21 years, cooper. Charles McLEOD, nephew, 15 years, fitter at foundry. Ann McLEOD, niece, 19 years, all born Scotland.

McDUFF John, 45 years, gardener, born Scotland. Living at 27 Lord Street Court, Bolton. 1871 census. With Jane, wife, 45 years, born Sestrington, Yorkshire. John, son, 10 years, born Manchester. Reel 4, 3925.

McGHIE John, 40 years, joiner, born Scotland. Living at 10 Garden Street, St. Andrews, Manchester. 1851 census. With Ellen, wife, 38 years, born Wales. Children, James, 9 years. John, 2 years. Mary, 7 years. Janet, 4 years, all born Manchester. Reel HO 107/2226, page 709a.

McGREGOR Alex., 35 years, unmarried, agricultural implement engineer, born Scotland. Lodging at house of Thomas HANDS. 13 Henry Street, Bedford, Leigh, Lancs. 1871 census.

McGREGOR living at 105 Simpsons court, Carlisle. 1851 census.
Jennet McGregor, married, 59 years. Ann, dau., unmarried, 35
years, roller coverer. Agnes, dau., unmarried, 25 years, dress
maker. Jannet, dau., 14 years, factory, all born Scotland.

MACHOLLAND James, 34 years, crown glass cutter, born Scotland.
Living at Westfield Street, Eccleston, St. Helens, Lancs. 1851
census. With Elizabeth, wife, 34 years. Betsy, dau., 16 years,
both born West Derby, Lancs.

McINNES Ramsay, 68 years, retired herald painter, born Scotland.
Living at 19 Clerendon Street, Hougham in Dover, Kent. 1881
census. With Emma, wife, 46 years, born Prussia B.S. Reel
RG11/1006.

MACKINTOSH John, unmarried, 28 years, railway labourer, born
Scotland. Lodging at Park Street, Hatfield, Herts. 1851 census.
Reel HO 107/1712, p. 5, folio 120, sch. 21.

MACKAY Stewart Ruthvin, died 1st May 1853 age 66 years. Thomas
ROBERTSON died 9th August 1853 age 52 years. Both natives of
Scotland and late residents in the Brazils, South America. St.
James, Liverpool.

McKENZIE Elizabeth, born 23rd February 1804, baptised 3rd June
1804, 3rd dau. of John McKenzie, mariner, native of North
Britain by his wife Isabella REED, native of this place. St.
Hilda's, South Shields, Co Durham, baptisms.

McKIE lodging at house of Matthew BUTTERWICK, Stokesley, North
Riding of Yorkshire. 1851 census. Sophia McKie, widow, 60 years,
seamstress. James, son, 30 years, both born Scotland.

MACKINNON Peter, married, 50 years, coastguard - Royal Navy,
born Scotland. Living at St. Margaret's Bay, Kent. 1861 census.
With Grace, wife, 49 years, born Scotland. Children, Daniel, 19
years, Royal Navy, born Foulness, Essex. Grace, 16 years. Adam,
14 years. Margaret, 10 years, all born St. Margaret's, Kent.
Jane MACCELLAND, mother, widow, 72 years, born Scotland. Reel.
RG 9/547, folio 52, page 11.

McKNIGHT Daniel, married, 69 years, master dyer, born Scotland.
Living at 178 Willow Holme, Carlisle. 1851 census. With,
Catherine, wife, 53 years, born Scotland. Children, James,
unmarried, 31 years, master woolen manu. employing 16 men. John,
unmarried, 30 years. Catherine PEARSON, dau., married, 23 years,
all born Carlisle.

McKNIGHT James, married, 44 years, dyer, born Scotland. Living
at 133 Denton Hill, Carlisle. 1851 census. With Sarah, wife, 43
years, born Scotland. Children, John, 24 years. Sarah, 20 years.
Mary Ann, 17 years. Nancy, 15 years. Isabella, 14 years. Eliz.,
11 years. Jane, 8 years. Martha, 1 year. James, 4 years, all
born Carlisle.

McKNO? William, 46 years, clothes dealer, born Scotland. Living at Winwick Street, Warrington. 1851 census. With Eleanor, wife, 46 years, born Stockport. Sam, son, 15 years, born Cullyford, Devon.

McLACHLAN William, married, 37 years, sawyer, born Scotland. Living at 58 Gibson Street, Newcastle upon Tyne. 1871 census, East All Saints. With Maria, wife, 31 years, born Axminster. Children, William, 10 years, born Newcastle. Walter, 6 years. Selina, 4 years, both born South Shields. Joseph, 2 years, born Newcastle.

McLEAN living at The Cotton Factory Yard, Township of Eccleston, St. Helens, Lancs. 1851 census. David McLean, 51 years, steam engine and machine fitter. Margaret, wife, 46 years. Children, David, 21 years, steam engine and machine fitter. James, 19 years, steam engine and machine fitter. Margaret, 18 years, house servant. Alexander, 13 years, ?stone potters? all born Scotland. John, 9 years, born Patricroft, Lancs. Isabella, 4 years, born St. Helens, Lancs.

McLEAN lodging at Nob Row, Bolton. 1851 census. Eliza McLean, unmarried, 19 years. Catherine McLean, unmarried, 16 years, both born Scotland. Reel 2211 2Cd, folio 581a and 582.

McLEAN William, married, 43 years, mate - MS, born Scotland. Living at Sailors home, 44 Stuart Street, Docks, Cardiff. 1881 census.

McLEOD nephews and niece of Angus McDOUGALL, see McDOUGALL Angus for details.

McLEOD living at 17 Industrial Dwellings, Newcastle upon Tyne. 1871 census, East All Saints. Alexander McLeod, married, 36 years, lithographic printer. Janet, wife, 33 years, both born Scotland. Children, Isabella M. 11 years. Ewen, 10 years, both born Newcastle. Catherine, 7 years. Mary, 5 years. Charlotte A. 3 years. Janet, 2 years. Margaret, 8 months, all born Scotland.

McMORRAN living at 62 Denton holme, Carlisle. 1851 census. Christiana McMorran, widow, 54 years, house w. Robert, son, 25 years, railguard. Mary, dau., 23 years. William, grandson, 3 years. Robert CARRUTHERS, nephew, 11 years, all born Scotland.

MACPHERSON John, burial Ovingham, Northumberland. 6th January 1784. A North Britain from Harlow Hill.

McQUEEN George, born 9th October 1802, baptised 25th April 1803, 3rd son of Alexander McQueen, mariner, native of North Britain, by his wife Mary McFARLEN, native of Kingsale, Ireland. St. Hilda's, South Shields, Co Durham, baptisms.

McRAE Farquhar, 32 years, Royal Engineer, born Scotland. Lodging at house of Richard MARKS, baker, Village, St, Margarets at Cliffe, Kent. 1861 census. With Janet, wife, 32 years, born Scotland.

McREY John, unmarried, 48 years, born Scotland. Visitor in house
of John ARMSTRONG, see same for further details.

McROY Mathew, married, 40 years, hawker of toys, born Scotland.
Lodging in house of Edward HUNT, see same, 16 Blue Anchor Lane,
Carlisle. 1851 census. With Margaret, wife, 41 years, born
Scotland.

McSKIMMING William? married, 40 years, carter, born Scotland.
Living at Caldcoats, Carlisle. 1851 census. With Euphemia, wife,
34 years, born Scotland. children, Charles, 9 years. John, 6
years. James, 3 years. Margaret, 10 months, all born Cumbria.

McTACE? Fanny, unmarried, 31 years, house sevant, born Scotland.
In house of Joseph ROBINSON, miller. 128 Denton Hill, Carlisle.
1851 census.

McTURK Alex. married, 56 years, born Scotland. Living at 179
Church Street, Carlisle. 1851 census. with Isabella, wife, 50
years, born Scotland. Children Jane, unmarried, 23 years.
Alexander, 18 years. Henry, 15 years, all born Carlisle.

McVAY lodging at house of Duncan KEAN, 32 Davies Street, St.
Philips, Manchester. 1851 census. Margaret McVay, 64? years,
widow, servant, born Scotland. Shuer McVay, married, dau! 34
years, born Scotland. Reel HO 107/2226 page 766.

McVICAR Alexander, married, 54 years, cabinet maker, born
Scotland. Living at 22 Portugal Street, Ancoats, Manchester.
1881 census. With Esther, wife, 59 years, born Hyde, Cheshire.
Reel 2855 Dist. 11.

McWHAN living at 153 Bread Street, Carlisle. 1851 census.
Caldergate Trinity, folio 323, page 37. James McWhan, married,
39 years, lab. saw mill. Jane, wife, 42 years. Children, James,
17 years, lab. biscuit factory. Jeffery, 15 years, lab. biscuit
factory, all born Scotland. Mary, 5 years. Joseph, 3 years.
Robert, 5 months, all born Carlisle.

McWHINNIE James, 67 years, bookseller, born Scotland. Living at
55 Stock Street, St. Thomas, Manchester. 1851 census. With
Harriet, 45 years, wife, born Manchester. Alexander, widower, 88
years, former watchmaker, born Liverpool. Margaret B., sister,
58 years, born Scotland. David J. WEIR, nephew, 16 years, appr.
printer, born Scotland. Jessie H. REID, niece, 14 years,
milliner, born Scotland. Reel 2229.

NAPPER Isabella, born 9th March 1804, baptised 6th May 1804, 1st
dau. of James Napper, mariner, native of North Britain by his
wife Isabella BEST, native of Durham. St. Hilda's, South
Shields, Co Durham, baptisms.

NELSON Thomas, married, 43 years, builder, born Scotland. Living
at 169 Murrell Hill, Carlisle. 1851 census. With Juli S., wife,
33 years. Children, M.L., dau., 10 years. T.B., son, 9 years.
James, 7 years. Eliza, 5 years. John, 4 years. Isabella, 2
years. Ann, 1 year, all born Carlisle.

NELSON Andrew, married, 33 years, weaver, born Scotland. Living
at 139 Jane Street, Carlisle. 1851 census. With Sarah, wife, 39
years, born Carlisle.

NEWTON living at 198 Willow Holme, Carlisle. 1851 census. John
Newton, married, 35 years, dyer, born Scotland. Jane, wife, 35
years, born Carlisle. Children, William, 13 years, born
Scotland. Elizabeth, 8 years. Hannah, 1 year, both born
Carlisle.

NIMONS living at 213 Pattinson Lane, Carlisle. 1851 census.
William Nimons, married, 48 years, weaver. Ann, wife, 46 years,
winder, both born Ireland. Children, William, 20 years, weaver.
Edward, 18 years, weaver. Robert, 16 years, weaver, all born
Scotland.

NOBLE James, married, 27 years, baker, born Scotland. Living at
26 Blagdon Street, Newcastle upon Tyne. 1871 census, East All
Saints. With Lizzie, wife, 29 years. Alexander, son, 5 years,
both born Scotland.

ORANGE James, 48 years, paper hanger, born Scotland. Living at
11 Half Street, Cathedral, Manchester. 1851 census. With Susan,
34 years, presumed wife? born Halifax. Thomas, 21 years,
presumed son? by previous wife, born Leeds. Reel HO 107/2229 P.
225.

O'REEGAN living at 15 Chapel Buildings, Newcastle upon Tyne.
1871 census, East All Saints. Michael O'Reegan, married, 43
years, labourer - Chelsea pensioner, born Ireland. Ann, wife, 39
years, born Scotland. Children, John James, 17 years, moulder,
born Scotland. Sarah Ann, 13 years, born Maritius, pt. of
France. Jane, 8 years, born Bombay, East India. William Michael,
4 years. Isabella, 1 year, both born Newcastle.

ORMISTON Jane, 22 years, general domestic servant, born
Scotland. Sister in Law of David HEDLEY. 7 Bedford Street,
Newcastle upon Tyne. 1871 census, East All Saints. Rest of
household as follows. David HEDLEY, head, married, 30 years,
masons labourer, born Newcastle. Thomasine, wife, 30 years, born
Newcastle. Jane, dau., 10 years, born Newcastle. William, son, 1
year, born Newcastle. Catherine, mother, widow, 68 years,
labourer - attends market, born Scotland.

PARKER Elizabeth, born 5th March 1805, baptised 17th March 1805,
1st dau. of Joseph Parker, schoolmaster, native of North
Britain, by his wife Rosanna SWANEY?, native of Ireland. St.
Hilda's, South Shields, Co Durham, bpatisms.

PATON Thomas, 33 years, railway engineer, born Scotland. Living
at Mill Street, Warrington. 1851 census. With Mary, wife, ??
years, born Scotland. Children, Eliz., ?? years, born Ireland.
William, 7 years. Thomas, 2 years, both born Liverpool. Agnes, 3
months, born Warrington.

PEMBERTON Alexander, 41 years, manager of crown glass works, born Scotland. Living at Westfield Street, Eccleston. St. Helens. Lancs. 1851 census. With Ann, wife, 41 years, born Wakefield, Yorkshire. Children, Jane, 20 years, teacher infant school, born Lofthouse Gate, Yorkshire. John, 18 years, glass cutter. Samuel, 14 years, glass maker app., both born St. Helens, Lancs. Frances, 13 years. Anthony, 10 years. Hannah, 9 years. Sarah, 7 years. Alexander, 6 years. Joseph, 3 years. George, 1 year, all born West Derby, Lancs. Edward, 7 months, born St. Helens, Lancs. Thomas, brother, married, 27 years, born Hanslett, Yorkshire.

PEMBERTON Richard, 22 years, glass maker, born Scotland. Living at Westfield Street, Eccleston, St. Helens, Lancs. 1851 census. With Hannah, wife, 22 years, born St. Helens, Lancs.

PHILLIPS living at Union Row, Westbrook, Margate, Kent. 1841 census. St. John the baptist. Richard Phillips, 45, navy coastgaurd. Jane, 50 years, both not born Kent. Mary, 15 years, born Scotland. Susanna, 10 years, not born Kent. Reel HO 107/468 folio 31, page 16.

PHILLIPS Robert, 46 years, weaver, born Scotland. Living at 2 Gough Court, St. Thomas, Manchester. 1851 census. With Charlotte, wife, 42 years. James, son, 11 years, both born Kendal. Reel 2229.

POLLOCK living at 29 Gaythrops Lane, Carlisle. 1851 census. Hugh Pollock, married, 50 years, tin smith. Ann, wife, 41 years, both born Ireland. Children, Ann, 11 years. Esther, 11 years. William, 9 years. Jessy, 7 years. Janie, 2 years, all born Scotland.

PORTEUS Penelope, born 12th December 1804, baptised 21st April 1805, 2nd dau. of Henry Porteus, mariner, native of North Britain, by his wife, Elizabeth ROBSON, native of this place. St. Hilda's, South Shields, Co Durham, baptisms.

PORTEOUS William, married, 35 years, sawyer, born Scotland. Living at Caldcoats, Carlisle. 1851 census, Caldergate Trinity. With Elizabeth, wife, 28 years, born Scotland.

POTTS living at 220 Pattinsons Lane, Carlisle. 1851 census. Robert Potts, married, 45 years, weaver, born Kirkbampton, Cmb. Eleanor, wife, 40 years, weaver. Mary, dau., 9 years. William, son, 5 years, all born Scotland. Elizabeth, dau., 4 months, born Carlisle.

PURVES Thomas, 56 years, blacksmith, born Scotland. Living at 74 Every Street, All Soul's, Manchester. 1851 census. Reel HO 107/2226, page 684. With Eliz., wife, 46 years. Children, Ann, 15 years. Mary Phillips, 13 years. Robert, 11 years, all born Manchester. Peter St. Scottish Church registers, have wife's name as Eliz. PHILLIPS.

PURVIS James, unmar, 19 yrs. joiner jour. born Scotland. Lodging at Westfield Street, Eccleston, St. Helens, Lancs. 1851 census.

PYAT James, unmarried, 29 years, cabinet maker, born Scotland. Living at 30 Back Spring Gardens, Bolton. 1851 census. Reel 2211 IL, folio 417a.

QUIN living at 8 Gaythrops Lane, Carlisle. 1851 census. Caldergate Trinity, folio 305, page 1. Robert Quin, married, 40 years, tallow chandler, born Scotland. Eilzabeth, wife, 34 years, born Hayton, Cum. Charles, son, 15 years, painter, born Scotland.

QUIN living at Parkham Beck, Carlisle. 1851 census. Terence Quin, married, 55 years, weaver, born Ireland. Thomas, son, unmarried, 30 years, weaver. Frances, dau., unmarried, 19 years, winder. Jane, dau., unmarried, 17 years, weaver, all born Scotland.

RAMSEY George, 38 years, coachplater, born Scotland. Living at 29 Kennedy Street, St. Ann's, Manchester. 1851 census. With Eliz., wife, 34 years, born Frodsham, Cheshire. Mary, dau., 13 years, born Manchester. Alice CONNELEY, niece, 7 years, born Frodsham, Cheshire. Reel 2229.

REA living at 69 Byron Street, Carlisle. 1851 census. Nancy Rea, widow, 70 years, born Scotland. Nancy, dau., 38 years, married, born Scotland. John, grandson, 11 years, born Scotland. Mary, granddau., 5 years, born Carlisle.

REID living at 21 Blagdon Street, Newcastle upon Tyne. 1871 census, East All Saints. Elizabeth Reid, widow, 56 years, born Berwick on Tweed. Children, James, 24 years, unmarried, striker, born Berwick on Tweed. Helen, 20 years, unmarried, assists at home. Philip, 18 years, unmarried, printer compositor, both born Scotland. Thomas, 8 months, born Newcastle.

REID Jessie H., niece of James McWHINNIE, see McWHINNIE James for details.

REID William, married, 39 years, weaver cotton, born Scotland. Living at 22 Chambers Court, Carlisle. 1851 census. With Mary, wife, 41 years, weaver cotton. Children, John, 7 years. James, 2 years, all born Carlisle.

REID John, 58 years, banker, born Scotland. Living at Bank of England Branch, King Street, Manchester. 1851 census. With, Adelaide, wife, 49 years, born London. Children, John Herbert, 19 years. Augusta Charlotte, 17 years. Thomas Maitland, 15 years. Samuel Grant, 13 years. Emily M---? 10 years, all born Manchester. Also Lt. Col. David HAY, visitor, 57 years, 6th Dragoon Guards, married, born EDINBURGH. Reel 2229.

RICHARDSON Peter, 22 years, unmarried, tailor, born Scotland. Lodging at 14 Velvet Walk, Bolton. 1851 census. Reel 2211 IK, folio 363a.

RICHEY Peter, born 16th Feb. 1802, bapt. 5th Feb. 1804, 5th son of Alexander Richey, mariner, of North Britain, by his wife Julia SCORAY, of Swallwell. St. Hilda's, South Shields, bapt.

ROBERTSON Thomas, married, 28 years, weaver, born Scotland.
Living at 54 Denton Holme, Carlisle. 1851 census, Caldergate
Trinity, folio 375, page 12. With Jannet, wife, 20 years, born
Scotland.

ROBERTSON Thomas, on same M.I. as Stewart Ruthvin MACKAY, see
same for details.

ROBERTSON Peter, married, 50 years, able seaman, born Scotland.
Living at Sailors Home, 44 Stuart Street, Docks, Cardiff. 1881
census.

ROBERTSON Alexander, 38 years, tailor, born Scotland. Living at
10 Kennedy Street, St. Ann's, Manchester. 1851 census. With
Jessie, wife, 32 years, born Scotland. Helena, 3 years, dau.,
born Manchester. Reel 2229.

ROBINSON Elizabeth, dau., of William BOND, see same for details.

ROBSON or FARRER, John, born 29th November 1803, baptised 16th
June 1805, illegitimate son of Thomas Robson, boat builder,
native of this place, by Isabella FARRER, native of North
Britain. St. Hilda's, South Shields, Co Durham, baptisms.

ROME? or RONIE? living at 94 Simpsons Court, Carlisle. 1851
census. Ann, widow, 85 years, born Scotland. Margaret,
granddau., unmarried, 20 years, dress maker, born Scotland.

RUTHERFORD Richard, 40 years, clerk in cotton factory, born
Scotland. Living at 5 Reynor Street, St. James, Manchester. 1851
census, reel 2229. With Isabella, wife, 33 years, born Scotland.

RUTHERFORD Martin C. married, 27 years, joiner, born Scotland.
Living at 31 Industrial Dwellings, Newcastle upon Tyne. 1871
census, East All Saints. With Jessie, wife, 26 years. Isabella,
dau., 3 years. Catherine, dau., 1 year, all born Scotland.

RYLEY Patrick, unmarried, 20 years, hawker of smallware, born
Scotland. Visitor in house of Edward HUNT, see same for futher
details.

SCHULLEY Francis, 34 years, unmarried, able seaman, born
Scotland. Living at Sailors Home, 44 Stuart Street, Docks,
Cardiff. 1881 census.

SCOBIE David, 52 years, earthenware dealer and joiner, born
Scotland. Living at 52 Portland Street, St. James, Manchester.
1851 census, reel 2229. With Ann, wife, 44 years. Ellen, dau., 7
years, both born Manchester.

SCOTT John, unmarried, 32 years, weaver, born Scotland. Lodging
at 160 Chappel Lane, Carlisle. 1851 census. House of Jane
MILLBURN.

SCOTT living at Caldcoats, Carlisle. 1851 census, Caldergate
Trinity, page 9. William Scott, married, 38 years, weaver, born
Cumbria. Sarah, wife, 30 years, hawker. Margaret, dau., 10
years. William, 5 years, all born Scotland.

SCOTT William, married, 24 years, hawker of crockery, born
Scotland. Visitor in house of William INGHAM, 89 Bridge Lane,
Carlisle. 1851 census. With Ann, wife, 24 years, born Scotland.

SCOTT William, 31 years, ship lamp maker, born Scotland. Living
at 25 Buxton Street, Newcastle upon tyne. 1871 census East All
Saints. With Mary, wife, 31 years, born Scotland. Margaret
FRANCE, sister in law, 17 years, bookfolder, born Scotland.

SEATON James, 66 years, joiner, born Scotland. Living at 11 Back
Copestick Street, All Souls, Manchester. 1851 census. With Jane,
wife, 65 Years, born Scotland. Children, Mary, 16 years, born
Scotland. James, 14 years. Jane, 7 years, both born Manchester.
Reel HO 107/2226 page 698/698a.

SEATON living at 225 Pattinsons Lane, Carlisle. 1851 census.
William Seaton, married, 62 years, weaver. Mary, wife, 57 years.
Children, Jessie, unmarried, 27 years, factory w. Johnathan,
unmarried, 22 years. Margaret WALLACE, dau., married, 18 years,
bobbin winder. Phebe Seaton, dau., 14 years, bakehouse. William
BELL, grandson in law, 14 years, piecer. John Seaton, grandson,
7 years. Jane Seaton, granddau., 5 years, all born Scotland.

SHAN or SLOAN Alexander, widower, 74 years, labourer, born
Scotland. Living at 116 Brewery Row, Carlisle. 1851 census,
Caldergate Trinity, folio 382, page 25. With Ann, dau.,
unmarried, 32 years, born Scotland.

SHARP Henry, born October 1804, baptised 10th January 1805, 1st
son of William Sharp, native of North Britain, by his wife Ann
MADISON, native of this place. St. Hilda's, South Shields, Co
Durham, baptisms.

SHAW George, 26 years, machinist, born Scotland. Living at 17
St. James Street, Manchester. 1851 census, reel 2229. With
Margaret, wife, 28 years, born Scotland. James, son, 4 years,
born Manchester.

SHILLINGLAW living at 34 Back? Blagdon Street, Newcastle upon
Tyne. 1871 census, East All Saints. Richard Shillinglaw,
married, 44 years, cartman. Janet Brown Shillinglaw, wife, 48
years. Children, Cristina, 17 years, millworker. William, 14
years, slater. Alexandrina, 11 years, all born Scotland.

SHILLINGLAW John, married, 19 years, cartman, born Scotland.
Living at 9 Grenville Terrace, Newcastle upon Tyne. 1871 census,
East All Saints. With Mary Ann, wife, 21 years, born Scotland.

SHORT David, 76 years, silversmith's porter, born Scotland.
Living at Lendal Chapel Yard, St. Martin's, York. 1851 census.
With Margaret, wife, 66 years, born York.

SIMON Mary, born 22nd March 1804, baptised 15th July 1804, 1st
dau. of David Simon, labourer, native of North Britain, by his
wife, Ann DICKINSON, native of Evenwood, Durham. St. Hilda's,
South Shields, Co Durham, baptisms.

SIMPSON living at Stokesley, North Riding of Yorkshire. 1851
census. Francis Simpson, married, 28 years, bookbinder. Mary,
wife, 30 years. George, son, 6 years, all born Scotland.

SIMPSON living at Caldcoats, Carlisle. 1851 census. John
Simpson, married, 35 years, tanner, born Carlisle. Margaret,
wife, 30 years, born Scotland. Children, Mary, 3 years. Joseph,
1 year, both born Scotland.

SINCLAIR Elizabeth, niece of James CUNNINGHAM, see same for
details.

SLOAN? or SHAN? see SHAN? or SLOAN? Alexander for details.

SMITH living at 3 Groom? Street, St. Philips, Manchester. 1851
census. David Smith, 50 years, mechanic fitter. Mary, wife, 42
years. Children, Charles, 20 years. Ann, 13 years. Thomas, 10
years, all born Scotland. Reel HO 107/2229, page 766a.

SMITH John, married, 42 years, carter, born Scotland. Living at
212 Pattinsons Lane, Carlisle. 1851 census, Caldergate Trinity,
folio 330, page 51. With Mary, wife, 42 years, born Bristol.
Children, Allace, 19 years. John, 14 years. Henry, 11 years.
William BLACKLOCK, grandson, all born Carlisle.

SMITH living at Eccleston Street, Eccleston, St. Helens, Lancs.
1851 census. Benjamin Smith, 30 years, glass flint maker.
Sarah, wife, 26 years. Benjamin, son, 3 years, all born
Scotland. Elizabeth, dau., 11 months, born St. Helens, Lancs.

SMITH lodging at Eccleston Street, Eccleston, St. Helens, Lancs.
1851 census. Alexander Smith, unmarried, 19 years, journeyman
tailor. John McINTYRE, unmarried, 24 years, journeyman tailor,
both born Scotland.

SMITH Robert, married, 49 years, labourer, born Scotland. Living
at Caldcoats, Carlisle. 1851 census. With Mary, wife, 45 years,
born Cumbria. Children, Thomas, 25 years. Elizabeth, 18 years.
Joseph, 15 years. Isaac, 12 years. Robert, 9 years, all born
Cumbria.

SMITH living at Caldcoats, Carlisle. 1851 census. James Smith,
married, 61 years, sawyer. Catherine, wife, 59 years. Thomas,
son, 15 years, all born Scotland.

SMITH living at 110 Jane or June Street, Carlisle. 1851 census.
John Smith, married, 38 years, boot and shoe maker. Elizabeth,
wife, 40 years, dressmaker. John, son, 10 years, all born
Scotland.

SMITH David, born October 1804, baptised 9th December 1804, 3rd
son of James Smith, labourer, native of North Britain, by his
wife Jane WEIGHTON, native of North Britain. St. Hilda's, South
Shields, Co Durham, baptisms.

SMITH living at 2 Chapel Building, Newcastle upon Tyne. 1871
census, East All Saints. William Smith, married, 43 years,
labourer, born Ireland. Sarah, wife, 27 years, pedlar, born
Scotland. Children, John, 8 years. Mary, 6 years. Thomas, 4
years. Sarah, 8? years, all born Scotland.

SMITH living at 163 Chappel Lane, Carlisle. 1851 census. John
Smith, married, 25 years, weaver. Mary Ann, wife, 26 years,
weaver. Martha, dau., 4 years. Mary, dau., 2 years, all born
Scotland.

SOMERVILLE Thomas, Dr. of law. In 1851 census, Wilmslow, reel
2768, E3c, age 44 years, schoolteacher - farmer, born Scotland.
Mary Maria (nee COCHRANE), wife, age 40 years, born Tamworth,
Staffs. Children, Lillian, 16 years. Wallace, 14 years, both
born Rowley Regis. James, 7 years. Elizabeth, 6 years. Thomas
Alex., 4 years. Agnes, 2 years. Emily, 6 months, all born
Wilmslow. Frank Linn Somerville was born in Wilmslow in 1854.

SOWERBY John, married, 66 years, poulterer, born Scotland.
Living at 37 Denton Holme, Carlisle. 1851 census. With Eliz.,
wife, 61 years, born Carlisle.

SPENCE Thomas, married, 44 years, weaver, born Scotland. Living
at 192 Willow Holme, Carlisle. 1851 census. With Elizabeth,
wife, 35 years, born Scotland. John, son, 5 years. Thomasina, 3
years, both born Wigton.

SPENSAR Barbary, married, 21 years, ropemaker, born Scotland.
Living at Chorley, (town), Lancs. 1851 census, reel 2263, folio
104.

STEEN James, married, 50 years, warehouseman, born Scotland.
Living at Caldcoats, Carlisle. 1851 census. With Margaret, wife,
42 years, born Durham. Margaret, dau., 15 years. Elizabeth,
dau., 12 years, both born Carlisle.

STEEN Jane, married, 80 years, born Scotland. Living at
Caldcoats, Carlisle. 1851 census. With Adam, son, married, 36
years. James, grandson, unmarried, 23 years. Thomas, grandson,
17 years, all born Carlisle.

STEWART lodging at 41 Bradford Road, Manchester. House of Eliz.
McVOY, 1851 census. George Stewart, 29 years, unmarried, piecer.
Hugh Stewart, 24 years, unmarried, piecer, both born Scotland.

STEWART James, widower, 58 years, weaver, born Scotland. Living
with William O'HAIR, relative, Parkham Beck, Carlisle. 1851
census.

STEWART George, married, 27 years, seaman, born Scotland. Living
at 44 Industrial Dwellings, Newcastle upon tyne. 1871 census,
East All Saints. With, Eliza, wife, 32 years, born Somerset,
Bristol. Also following step-children, Elizabeth HAYDON, 12
years. Harriet Haydon, 9 years, both born Somerset, Bristol.
Robert Haydon, 6 years, born South Shields, Durham.

STEWART lodging in house of Mary WALKER, (see WALKER), 48 Gibson
Street, Newcastle upon Tyne. 1871 census, East All Saints.
Thomas Stewart, 27 years, cartman. Peter M. Stewart, 24 years,
cellarman, both born Scotland.

STODDART Robert, married, 45 years, warper, born Scotland.
Living at 101 Brewery Row, Carlisle. 1851 census. With Margaret,
wife, 39 years, born Carlisle. Children, James, 8 years. Mary, 4
years. Dinah, 10 months, all born Carlisle.

STORY James, married, 60 years, cott. weaver, born Scotland.
Living at 87 Bridge Street, Carlisle. 1851 census. With Ann,
wife, 53 years, born Carlisle. Children, Thomas, 21 years.
James, 18 years. Ann, 15 years. Henry, married, 27 years,
weaver. Margaret, son's wife, 24 years, bobbin w. Ann,
granddau., 5 years. Mary, granddau., 3 years, all born Carlisle.

STOTT James, 25 years, confectioner, born Scotland. Living at
Marygate, York. 1851 census. With Sarah, wife, 22 years. James,
son, 2 years, both born York.

STRONACH Henry, married, 64 years, cabinet maker, born Scotland.
Living at 8 Grenville Terrace, Newcastle upon Tyne. 1871 census,
East All Saints. With, Ann, wife, 63 years, blind, born
Newcastle. Thomas, son, unmarried, 26 years, labourer in guano
works. George FARRIER, brother in law, widower, 68 years,
cabinet maker. Hannah WALKER, niece, unmarried, 19 years,
domestic servant. George NIXON, nephew, 13 years, all born
Newcastle.

STUART Mary, unmarried, 25 years, born Scotland. Servant in
house of John HATCH. Bay, St. Margaret's at Cliffe, Kent. 1851
census. Reel HO 107/1632, folio 68, page 13.

SUTHERLAND James, married, 55 years, shipwright, born Scotland.
Living at 29 Industrial Dwellings, Newcastle upon tyne. 1871
census, East All Saints. With Eliza, wife, 50 years, born
Scotland.

SWAN Peter, widower, 41 years, earthenware dealer, born
Scotland. Living at 242 Oldham Road, Ancoats, Manchester. 1881
census. With Mary, dau., 17 years. James, nephew, 15 years, both
born Manchester. Reel 2855, dist. 13.

THOMPSON david, married, 32 years, stonemason, born Scotland.
Living at Chorley (town), Lancs. 1851 census. Reel 2263, folio
100.

THOMPSON Robert, 49 years, private teacher, born Scotland.
living at 123 Spring Gardens, Bolton. 1851 census. With
Catherine, wife, 52 years, born Stowe, Staffordshire. Reel 2211,
IL, folio 414.

THOMPSON Philip, 45 years, bank manager, born Scotland. Living
at 27 Spring Gardens, St. Ann's, Manchester. 1851 census. With
Jessie, wife, 50 years, born Scotland. Children, John James, 17
years, banker's clerk. Jessie, 16 years. Philip, 15 years. Jane
Ellen, 12 years. Dora, 10 years, all born Manchester. Reel 2229

TOMPSON John, 27 years, joiner, born Scotland. Living at 13 Lord
Street, St. Thomas, Manchester. 1851 census. With Mary, wife, 27
years, born Aldwash, Derby. Alex., brother, 17 years, engineer,
born Scotland. David, CANT, 18 years, lodger, joiner, born
Scotland. Reel 2229.

TOUGH living at 2 Victoria Place, Newcastle upon Tyne. 1871
census, East All Saints. James Tough, head, unmarried, 28 years,
bootmaker. Elizabeth, sister, unmarried, 30 years, housekeeper.
William, brother, 26 years, bootmaker. Daniel, brother, 21
years, bootmaker, all born Scotland.

TURNBULL John, married, 73 years, watch maker, born Scotland.
Living at Stokesley, North Riding of Yorkshire. 1851 census.
With Ann, wife, 73 years, born Stockton.

TURNER James, unmarried, 21 years, tailor, born Scotland.
Lodging in house of Dommick HANDY, 96 Hill Street, St. Philip,
Birmingham. 1851 census. En. 10, sch. 142, page 326.

TWEDDIE James, married, 42 years, cotton w., born Scotland.
Living at Caldcoats, Carlisle. 1851 census. With Jane, wife, 45
years, born Cumbria.

TYSON Elizabeth, unmarried, 31 years, born Scotland. House
servant in 15 Upton House, Canford, St. Mary's, Longfleet, Poole
area, Dorset. 1851 census.

VALLENTINE living at 4 Bedford Sreet, Newcastle upon Tyne. 1871
census, East All Saints. Elizabeth Vallentine, head, unmarried,
25 years, dressmaker. Jessie, sister, unmarried, 21 years,
weaver. Georgina, sister, 17 years, all born Scotland. Elizabeth
JAMES, visitor, 21 years, spinner, born Scotland. Isabella
James, visitor, 1 year, born France, British subject.

VERNON Alexander, married, 30 years, tea dealer, born Scotland.
Living at 129 Wimborne Road, Longfleet, Poole area, Dorset. 1851
census. With (Cu)phemia, mother, widow, 73 years, housekeeper,
born Scotland. Children, John M., 2 years. Mary M., 1 year, both
born Longfleet, Dorset. Reel HO 107, box 7, 1-268.

VERNON James, married, 42 yrs. British manu. master employing 12
men, born Scotland. Living at High Street, Poole area, Dorset.
With Ellen, wife, 34 yrs. born Southampton, Hants. Children,
Donald, 11 yrs. James, 10 yrs. Margaret E., 8 yrs. John, 6 yrs.
1851 census.

WALDIE living at 92 Simpsons Court, Carlisle. 1851 census. Peter
Waldie, married, 31 years, manager wool tailor. Cristina, wife,
32 years. Isabella, dau., 10 years. John, 8 years, all born
Scotland.

WALKER or BARKER Robert, born 6th March 1803, baptised 30th
March 1803, illegitimate son of Robert Walker, mariner, native
of Scotland, by Jane BARKER, native of Green Hammerton,
Yorkshire. St. Hilda's, South Shields, Co Durham, baptisms.

WALKER living at 52 Byron Street, Carlisle. 1851 census. Jn.
Walker, married, 35 years, shoe maker. Ellen, wife, 25 years.
Francis, son, 1 year 6 months, all born Scotland.

WALKER living at 48 Gibson Street, Newcastle upon Tyne. 1871
census, East All Saints. Mary Walker, head, widow, 49 years,
keeps lodgers. Agnes, dau., unmarried, 20 years, boot closer,
both born Scotland. Thomas, son, 8 years, born Newcastle.

WALKER James, married, 23 years, baker, born Scotland. Living at
Caldcoats, Carlisle. 1851 census. With Ann, wife, 18 years.
Charlotte, dau., 4 months, both born Carlisle.

WALKER John, unmarried, 25 years, born Scotland. Lodging in
house of Robert GRIERSON, Caldcoats, Carlisle. 1851 census.

WALKER Peter, 55 years, widower, bewer? born Scotland. Living at
King Street, Warrington. 1851 census. With Agnes, dau., 22
years, unmarried, born Scotland.

WALKER Jane, 14 years, born Scotland. Servant in house of George
A. GRANT (see same), 50 Gibson Street, Newcastle upon Tyne. 1871
census, East All Saints.

WALLACE John, married, 34 years, cotton weaver, born Scotland.
Living at 192 Pattinson Lane, Carlisle. 1851 census. With
Elizabeth, wife, 34 years, born Carlisle. Children, John, 12
years. Mary Ann, 9 years. William, 4 years. Sarah, 2 years, all
born Carlisle.

WALLACE John, married, 45 years, dyer, born Scotland. Living at
25 Gaythrops Lane, Carlisle. 1851 census. With Ann, wife, 35
years, born Carlisle. Children, Jno, 9 years. Samuel, 14 years.
Jane, 12 years. George, 10 years. Margaret, 2 years 6 months,
all born Carlisle. Also Sarah GLOVER, visitor, unmarried, 28
years, born Scotland.

WALLACE Margaret, dau. of William SEATON, see SEATON for
details.

WALLACE Jane, 15 years, scholar, born Scotland. Inmate of Garth
Heads Ragged and Industrial Schools, Newcastle upon Tyne. 1871
census, East All Saints.

WALLS living at 7 Grenville Terrace, Newcastle upon Tyne. 1871
census, East All Saints. William I. Walls, 40 years, labourer at
soap works, born Lanchester, Durham. Agnes I., wife, 37 years,
born Scotland. Children, George, 8 years, born Scotland. Mary, 6
years. William, 2 years, both born Newcastle.

WALTON John, 33 years, labourer and guano worker, born Scotland.
Living at 2 Tinners Entry, Pandon, Newcastle upon Tyne. 1871
census, East All Saints. With Elizabeth, wife, 32 years, born
Newcastle. Children, Mary A. 10 years, born Gateshead. George, 8
years. William, 6 years. John T. 4 years. Harriet, 1 year, all
born Newcastle.

WARNOCK Margaret, wife of Angus McCOLL, see same for details.

WATT Alexander, widower, 82 years, retired farmer, born
Scotland. Lodging at house of John LACEY, 15 Hill Street, St.
Philip, Birmingham. 1851 census. En. 12, sch. 17 page 373.

WEBSTER lodging in house of William HAY, see same, 33 Industrial
Dwellings, Newcastle upon Tyne. 1871 census. Samuel Webster,
unmarried, 25 years, joiner. James Webster, unmarried, 22 years,
both born Scotland.

WEIGHTON Jane, wife of James SMITH, see SMITH David for details.

WILLIAMSON Andrew, 37 years, Chelsea pensioner, born Scotland.
Boarding in house of Elizabeth TOUGH, see same, 2 Victoria
Place, Newcastle upon Tyne. 1871 census, East All Saints.

WILLIAMSON George, married, 54 years, printer, born Scotland.
Living at 43 Melbourne Street, Newcastle upon Tyne, 1871 census,
East All Saints. With Margaret, wife, 54 years, born Scotland.
Thomas, son, unmarried, 21 years, wireworker. Angus, son, 14
years, both born Newcastle.

WILSON Elizabeth, 20 years, born Scotland. Servant in house of
David RIPPON, 39 Melbourne Street, Newcastle upon Tyne. 1871
census, East All Saints.

WILSON William, married, 46 years, weaver, born Scotland. Living
at Parkham Beck, Carlisle. 1851 census. With, Jean, wife, 36
years, weaver, born Scotland.

WILSON Robert, unmarried, 21 years, born Scotland. Lodging in
house of Andrew NELSON, see same. 139 Jane Street, Carlisle.
1851 census.

WILSON George, married, 36 years, weaver, born Scotland. Living
at 146 Jane Street, Carlisle. 1851 census. With Elizabeth, wife,
29 years. John, son, 1 year, both born Carlisle.

WOOD living at 35 Melbourne Street, Newcastle-u-Tyne. 1871
census, East All Saints. Peter Wood, married, 29 yrs. tobacco
spinner. Mary, wife, 28 yrs. Children, Ellen, 10 yrs. Jane, 8
yrs. Robeina, 5 yrs. Margaret, 2 yrs. All born Scotland.

WREN William, married, 48 years, weaver, born Scotland. Living
at 219 Pattinsons Lane, Carlisle. 1851 census. With Margaret,
wife, 42 years, born Carlisle. John, son, 12 years, weaver, born
Carlisle. James ALLEN, visitor, 47 years, weaver, born Scotland.

WRIGHT George, married, 39 years, house servant, born Scotland.
Living at Stokesley, North Riding of Yorkshire. 1851 census.
With Elizabeth, wife, 40 years, born Stanhope, Durham. Children,
George, 4 years. Elizabeth, 3 years, both born Stokesley.

WYLIE Mary, unmarried, 36 years, servant, born Scotland. Living
at 10 Ridgeway Gates, Bolton. 1851 census. Reel 2211, IK, folio
367a.

WYLIE Thomas Philip, married, 32 years, born Scotland. Living at
Caldcoats, Carlisle. 1851 census. With Sarah, wife, 34 years.
Elizabeth, dau., 5 years, both born Carlisle.

YARKER? living at Parkham Beck, Carlisle. 1851 census. William
Yarker?, married, 27 years, tailor, born Westmoreland. Margaret,
wife, 25 years, born Scotland. Children, Elizabeth, 3 years.
Hellen, 7 months, both born Scotland.

YOUNG John, 43 years, millwright, born Scotland. Living at 15
Spring Gardens, Bolton. 1851 census. With Isabella, wife, 42
years, born Scotland. Children, Mary, 11 years, born Preston.
Isabella, 4 years, born Liverpool. Reel 2211, IL, folio 416.

HENNESSY Henry 45
HEPBURN J.(H).H. 55
HILL William 31
HIND Elizabeth 43
HUDSON Ann 13
HUGET Jennet 29
HUME Christian 19
HUMPHREY Isabella 10
HUNT 3,47,67
HUNTER Ann 32
HUNTER H.W. 11
HUNTER Isabella 38
HUNTER Martha 8
HUTTON 44

INGHAM William 72
ISMAY Thomas 42

JAMES 76
JEFFELS E. 5
JOHNSON I.(J).A. 40

KAYE Isabella 37
KEAN Duncan 67
KIRKPATRICK Rachel 43
KIRKTON Elizabeth 30
KNOWLES 19,23

LACEY John 78
LACK Jane 18
LAUDER M.(L).A. 16
LEDINGHAM Georgina 23
LEITCH A.N. 2
LIGHTFOOT Ann 42
LINN F.(L).S. 74
LONGSTAFF Joseph 19
LYON R.(L).D. 9

MACCELLAND Jane 65
McCORMICK Jane 59
McCURRICH James 4
McDERMOT Hugh 52
MACDONALD James 37
McFARLANE Margaret 43
McFARLEN Mary 66
McGARVIN Jane 35
McINTYRE John 73
McQUADE Elizabeth 34
McREY John 41
McTURK Alex. 55
McVOY Eliz. 74

MADISON Ann 72
MAIN George 51,54
MAITLAND T.(M).R. 70
MALCOLM Mary 32
MARKS Richard 66

MARQHIDORFF Sophia 37
MEABURN Anne 39
MILLBURN Jane 71
MILLER John 15
MILLER Georgiana 9
MINSHALL John 27
MITCHELL Ann 3
MOFFAT Corbat 31
MOONEY Patrick 60
MOORHEAD Mary 45
MORE A.(M).McF. 25
MORRIS John and William 19
MUIR Catherine 56
MURREY (M).L. 60

NEEL Ann 18
NELSON Andrew 45
NELSON Thomas 57
NIMONS William 50
NIXON David 41
NIXON George 75
NIXON Joseph 54
NOWELL Sibby 50

OATEN Elizabeth 20
O'CONNAL Patrick 63
O'HAIR William 74
OLIVER Christian 37
OLIVER Jane 9,49
ORD Ann 8
ORMOND Mary 53

PATTERSON Thomas 48
PATTINSON Dinah 9
PATTISON Sarah 2
PEACOCK Joseph 13
PEARSON Catherine 65
PEARSON Henry 15
PEET Mary 49
PETERKIN Grace 18
PHILLIPS Eliz. 69
POWRIE Adam 10
PUNSHOW Elizabeth 27

RALSTON J. 2
RAMSDEN Martha 45
RAMSEY Mary 9
RANDELL Joseph 44
REED Isabella 65
RENSHAW Mary Ann 53
RICHARDSON John F. 22
RIPPON David 78
ROBERTS Thomas 63
ROBERTSON F.W. 8
ROBINSON 42
ROBINSON Dorothy 47
ROBINSON Joseph 53,67

ROBSON Elizabeth   28,69
RONAY R.(R).D.   8
RONIE Ann   71
ROSS   14,21,40,44
ROW   56
RUSSELL James   61
RUTHVIN S.(R).M.   71

SCORAY Julia   70
SCOTT   6,26
SCOTT Margaret   47
SHARPE Mary   12
SHIELDS Mrs.   14
SINCLAIR   47,59
SKELTON John   35
SKIRVING Mr.   17
SMITH J.(S).B.   3
SMITH L.(S).R.   30
SMITH John   32
STALKHOUSE C.(S).R.   30
STEEL Margaret   35
STOKELL Eleanor   41
STOKEL? Jane   54
STORDY George   58
STRICKLAND H.(S).McC.   24
STROTHER Dr. W.J.   29
SWANEY Rosanna   68

TARSE Jane   37
TAYLOR Barbara   23
TAYLOR Grace   32
TENANT Sarah   20
THOBURN James   48
THOMAS George   15
THOMPSON William   32
TINDLE Thomasine   6
TIPLING Mary A.   49
TUCKER Elizabeth   34
TURNBULL E.(T).F.   10
TURNER Charlotte   11
TURNER Isaac   50
TUTEN Jane   6

UMPLEBY Rachael   50

VALENTINE Ann   10

WALKER Hannah   75
WARRINOR   29
WATSON Ann   29
WATSON Margaret   38
WATSON Mary   31
WEATHERALL J.(W).M.   24
WEIR David J.   67
WEISSE Maria   37
WHINHAM Elizabeth   50
WHITE   58

WHITE John   2
WIGHTON   33
WILBERFORCE Hannah   13,54
WILKINSON Ann   36
WILKINSON Mary   25
WILLIAMSON J.(W).H.   16
WILLIS   58
WREN William   40
WRIGHT Mary   6

YOUNG Frances   46

LETTERS IN BRACKETS e.g.
(G). INDICATE THAT THE
INDEXED NAME IS A FAMILY
SURNAME BEING USED AS A
CHRISTIAN NAME.

ANGLO SCOTTISH FAMILY HISTORY SOCIETY

The society was formed in November 1982 under the auspices of the Manchester & Lancashire Family History Society. Our principal aim is to promote the study of Scottish migrant families and to assist members with tracing their ancestors back to Scotland. Preservation of genealogical records is another major concern and to house our own collection the society has a library and study room in central Manchester. Here members may consult the latest Mormon microfiche - the International Genealogical Index (IGI), and the Old Parochial Registers of Scotland (OPR). Print-outs may be obtained on the premises or by post.

Facilities are shared by the parent society - the Manchester & Lancashire FHS, the Bolton & District FHS and the Anglo Scottish FHS. Regular meetings are held independently and are open to all members oh payment of the one annual subscription.

A quarterly Anglo Scottish Bulletin is issued to members with the M&LFHS Journal, "The Manchester Genealogist". For further details please contact the Honorary Secretary enclosing a SAE (British stamps) or International Reply Coupons.

Honorary Patron   Sir Guy Holland Bart.

Hon. Chairman   Mr J D Beckett, 34 Eastwood Avenue,
                         Droylsden, Manchester. M35 6BJ

Hon. Secretary   Mrs D F Ramsbotham, 10 Blantyre Road,
                         Swinton, Manchester. M27 1ER

Hon. Treasurer   Mr H King, 65 Taunton Road,
                         Ashton-under-Lyne, Lancs. OL7 9DR

Hon. Projects Officer   Miss V L Dixon, 36 Penrith Avenue,
                         Ashton-under-Lyne, Lancs. OL7 9JG

	U.K.	--OVERSEAS-- SURF.	AIR
Library Catalogue. ISBN 0 947701 07 9	£1.70	£1.80	£2.35
Library Catalogue (Supplement) ISBN 0 947701 27 3	£1.20	£1.30	£1.70
A Guide to the Registration Districts of Manchester ISBN 0 947701 01 X	£1.70	£1.80	£2.35
Parish & Non-Conformist Registers in Manchester Local History Library. ISBN 0 947701 12 5	£2.50	£2.60	£3.50
A Dictionary of Scottish Emigrants. Vol. 1 ISBN 0 9509494 0 X	£2.25	£2.30	£3.00
A Dictionary of Scottish Emigrants. Vol. 2 ISBN 0 947701 30 3	£2.50	£2.60	£3.50
Scottish Genealogy: A Digest of Library Sources ISBN 0 947701 10 9	50p	60p	£1.00
Directory of Members' Interests (Anglo Scottish FHS)	£1.70	£1.80	£2.35
Combined Register of Members' Interests 1986	£3.00	£3.20	£5.00
Lancashire Graveyards & Burial Grounds (new edition)	£1.95	£2.05	£2.25
Monumental Inscriptions of Whalley Parish Church (2 volumes) ISBN 1 870277 00 7	£4.00	£4.20	£5.70

1851 Census Surname Index of Manchester & Lancashire

Vol. 1 Newton, Beswick and Bradford HO 107/2231 ISBN 0 947701 00 1	£1.20	£1.30	£1.85
Vol. 2 Market Street Sub District HO 107/2229 ISBN 0 947701 02 8	£1.70	£1.80	£2.35
Vol. 3 London Road Sub District HO 107/2228 ISBN 0 947701 03 6	£1.70	£1.80	£2.35
Vol. 4 St.Georges Sub District HO 107/2230 ISBN 0 947701 04 4	£1.70	£1.80	£2.35
Vol. 5 Ancoats HO 107/2225-2226 ISBN 0 947701 28 1	£2.50	£2.60	£3.35
Vol. 7 Cheetham and Failsworth HO 107/2232 ISBN 0 947701 17 6	£1.70	£1.80	£2.35
Vol. 8 Hulme Sub District HO 107/2221 ISBN 0 947701 26 5	£2.00	£2.10	£2.65
Vol. 9 Didsbury & Ardwick Sub Distict HO 107/2219 ISBN 0 947701 25 7	£1.70	£1.80	£2.35
Vol.10 Chorlton on Medlock and Ardwick HO 107/2220 ISBN 0 947701 13 3	£1.70	£1.80	£2.35
Vol.11 Salford. HO 107/2222-2224 ISBN 0 947701 05 2	£2.00	£2.10	£2.65
Vol.12 Barton, Stretford and Worsley HO 107/2217-2218 ISBN 0 947701 06 0	£2.25	£2.30	£3.00
Vol.13 Droylsden, Audenshaw and Denton HO 107/2234-2235 ISBN 0 947701 09 5	£1.70	£1.80	£2.35
Vol.14 Standish & Aspull HO 107/2198 ISBN 0 947701 20 6	£1.70	£1.80	£2.35
Vol.15 Wigan HO 107/2199 ISBN 0 947701 21 4	£1.70	£1.80	£2.35
Vol.16 Hindley, Pemberton, Up-Holland & Ashton in Makerfield HO 107/2200-2201 ISBN 0 947701 19 2	£1.70	£1.80	£2.35
Vol.17 Leigh HO 107/2204-2205 ISBN 0 947701 22 2	£1.70	£1.80	£2.35
*Vol.21 Rochdale (Butterworth & Castleton Sub-districts) HO 107/2244 ISBN 1 870277 90 2	£1.45	£1.55	£1.80
*Vol.28 North Bury & Elton HO 107/2215 ISBN 1 870277 25 2	£1.95	£2.05	£2.25
*Vol.30 Haslingden (Newchurch Sub-district) HO 107/2248 ISBN 1 870277 85 6	£1.45	£1.55	£1.80
*Vol.32 Haslingden (Haslingden & Accrington Sub-districts) HO 107/2250 ISBN 1 870277 01 5	£1.95	£2.05	£2.25
*Vol.37 Blackburn (Western section) HO 107/2258 ISBN 1 870277 80 5	£1.45	£1.55	£1.80
*Vols 41/42 (combined vol.) Clitheroe (Whalley, Chipping, Gisburn & Slaidburn Sub-districts) and Stonyhurst College HO 107/2255 & 2256 ISBN 1 870227 06 6	£1.95	£2.05	£2.25
+Vol.43 Fylde (Kirkham, Lytham, & Poulton Le Fylde) HO 107/2269 ISBN 1 870227 11 2	£1.95	£2.05	£2.25

* Published by Lancashire FHHS   + Joint Publication

Available (post paid) from :- Manchester & Lancashire Family History Society,
3 Lytham Road, Manchester. M19 2AT.   Cheques/Postal Orders should be made
payable to "Manchester & Lancashire Family History Society".

U.S. $ checks accepted.